SPALDING.

SOCCER HANDBOOK

Paul Harris

MASTERS PRESS

A Subsidiary of Howard W. Sams & Co.

Published by Masters Press (a subsidiary of Howard W. Sams)
2647 Waterfront Pkwy E. Dr, Suite 300, Indianapolis, IN 46214

Printed in the United States of America

Cover photograph: Kent Phillips, Bloomington, Ind.

Library of Congress Cataloging-in-Publication Data
Harris, Paul E.

    Spalding soccer handbook / Paul Harris
        p. cm. -- (Spalding sports library. Soccer ; 1)
    ISBN 0-940279-46-0 : $9.95

    1. Soccer. 2.Soccer -- History. I. Title. II. Series.

  GV943.H313   1992   92-17842
  796.334--dc20   CIP

To Cynthia

"Come, my beloved, let us go into the country, let us spend the night in the villages."
—Song of Solomon 7:11 (NASB)

Acknowledgments

To Mark Montieth, editor at Masters Press, for reviewing and updating the text.

To the Major Soccer League; the National Professional Soccer League; the American Professional Soccer League; World Cup USA 1994, Inc.; and U.S. Soccer, for providing research material.

To the National Soccer Hall of Fame in Oneonta, N.Y.; the sports information department at St. Louis University; Sam Foulds; and Prof. Julio Mazzei, for providing photographs.

Contents

Preface

The word "football" means different things in different parts of the world. The average American sports fan thinks of the version peculiar to the United States that evolved from English rugby roots, with scrambling quarterbacks, blitzing linebackers and game-winning field goals. The Australians have their version, which is a combination of rugby, Gaelic football and soccer. The Irish have their Gaelic football with soccer overtones, and the British have both soccer and rugby.

The majority of people in the world, however, think of the game known in the U.S. as soccer when someone says "football." It is the most popular sport in the world, played and watched by more people than any other. As evidence, it is estimated that a combined audience of about 27 *billion* people watched the games of the 1990 World Cup on television, including an audience of more than one billion for the final game. In comparison, "only" 179.5 million people watched the 1991 Super Bowl.

Soccer has been slow to find a mass audience in the United States, but recent surveys indicate it is gradually catching on. About 14.5 million people six years or older played the game at least once in 1991, according to a survey released by the Soccer Industry Council of America. Players who participated 52 or more days a year totalled nearly 2.7 million, a 19 percent increase over 1987.

Among team sports, soccer ranks third in popularity in the United States (behind basketball and volleyball) for children under 18, and ranks second to basketball for children under 12.

The increased participation has led to improved results in international competition. In fact, 1991 was the most successful year ever for U.S. teams. The men's and women's national teams won the CONCACAF (Confederation Norte-Centroamericana y del Caribe de Futbol) championship — a competition between countries in North America, Central America and the Carribean — the under-23 men's team won the Pan American Games gold medal and the U.S. team won the first women's world championship in China.

The greatest moment for soccer in the United States, however, is yet to come. The World Cup will be played here for the first time in the summer of 1994, bringing the world's greatest talent to this country for an entire month, and is expected to propel soccer to unprecedented popularity in the U.S.

This volume of the Spalding Sports Library soccer series will help you to better understand this booming sport.

Part I: History

1

Pasuckquakkohowog, Anyone?

The origin of soccer is uncertain. Kicking about a round object is such a basic form of recreation that it no doubt was practiced in some form or other by people all over the world going back more than 2,000 years. The invention of soccer, therefore, has been credited to the Chinese, the Romans, the Greeks, the Egyptians and many others. All of them in ancient times might have played something roughly similar to the game people know today, but it is impossible to determine exactly when and where the game began.

Actually, it did not begin anywhere. Many versions of a kicking game have been played throughout history, and they gradually merged into a common form in the 19th century.

The Italians around 200 A.D., for example, played a game called *harpastum*, using a hair-filled ball. It is not clear whether the ball was played with the hands or feet, but the Italians are said to have introduced the game to Britain.

The British, however, probably were already playing a similar game. British soldiers are said to have played a kicking game with the skulls of the Roman soldiers they had defeated in A.D. 217. Still, the British kept the game alive and refined it more than anyone else over the following centuries.

The first mention of a soccer-like game in English literature is found in *A History of London*, written by William Fitzstephen in 1174. It was played by all segments of the population, rich and poor alike, and continued to grow in popularity for more than 200 years. The game became rougher and rougher, however, as towns divided into teams and village took on village for games played in open fields or on city streets. Finally, in 1314, King Edward II ordered the citizens in London to stop playing the game because he thought it was distracting them from more important matters, such as defending the country in battle. He decreed:

> "Forasmuch as there is great noise in the city caused by hustling over large balls from which many evils might arise which God forbid; we command and forbid on behalf of the King, on pain of imprisonment, such game to be used in the city in future."

The King's edict had little effect on the populace. King Edward III later tried banning the game in all of England in 1349 because he wanted the people to spend their free time on archery practice to better defend the country from invaders. Still, the game continued. Forty years later, Richard II issued a similar ban. Henry IV tried to keep people from playing the game at the start of the 15th century, as did various Scottish kings of that era and later monarchs.

Football, however, would not die.

About 1500, the Italians were playing a game called *calcio*, which featured 27 or more people on each side, with the object of kicking, passing, or carrying a ball across a goal line. The game was violent and often resulted in total bedlam, but it did resemble the modern version of the game.

The same was true in England, where the citizens continued to play despite orders to the contrary. The game the English played at that time lasted for several hours, perhaps all day, and was played between goals one-half mile or more apart. In 1572, Queen Elizabeth I banned the game in London. She received a great deal of support in this decree from noblemen and writers of the time, who provided insight into the game as it was then played. One writer reported:

> "Concerning football playing, I protest to you it may rather be called a friendly kind of fighting than recreation. For, does not every one lie in wait for his adversary to overthrow him and drop him on his nose, though it be on hard stones, in ditch or dale, or whatsoever place it may be he cares not, as long as he has him down. And he that can do this best, he is the player who counts. So that by this means sometimes their necks are broken, sometimes their backs or legs, sometimes their noses gush out blood and sometimes their eyes are put out. And no wonder, for they hit him against the heart with their elbows, butt him under the ribs with their fists and a hundred such other murderous devices."

Football became officially legal again in England in 1605. By the end of the 17th century, it was the country's most popular sport.

• • •

Soccer's origin in the United States is equally vague. The native Indians, however, played a game called "Pasuckquakkohowog," which in English can be translated to "They gather to play football," before the first Pilgrims landed at Plymouth Rock in 1620.

Charles C. Willoughby, in his *Commonwealth History of Massachusetts*, wrote that "football" was one of the favorite pastimes of the Indians. William Wood, an early settler in Massachusetts, also wrote about the game in his *New England Prospect* in 1634:

> "Apparently, the tribes of New England were the only Indians on the continent of North America who played this type of ball game. Usually, the Indians played football during the summer months with a varying number of players involved, depending upon the circumstances. Village played against village and a large amount of property changed hands, depending upon the outcome of the game. Surprisingly there was little quarreling."

The game usually was played on a broad, sandy beach at Lynn, Revere or Cape Cod, where areas as large as a mile long and a half-mile wide were available at low tide. Goal posts were placed at each end of the playing area, sometimes as much as a mile apart. The football was about the size of a handball. It had a cover of deerskin, and was stuffed with deer hair.

The Indians were very quick and agile. Wood was impressed with their "swift footmanship, their strange manipulation of the ball and their plunging into the water to wrestle for the ball," but he was not impressed with their technique or their strategy. He boasted that "one Englishman could beat ten Indians at football."

The teams often included 30-40 men on a side, but as many as 1,000 might play. Instead of donning a uniform, the Indians covered themselves with paint and ornaments as if preparing for battle. This way, nobody could be identified. It was not uncommon for bones to be broken during the course of a game, and the disguise prevented the player responsible for the injury from being identified and reduced the chances of retaliation.

The players hung their weapons on the nearby tree branches before the game, and shook hands over a line drawn in the sand across the middle of the playing area. For an important contest, the goal posts were laden with trophies such as wampum, beaver, otter and other skins. "It would exceed the belief of many to relate the worth of one goal," Wood wrote.

A festive atmosphere surrounded the important games, although the gaiety was foreign to the English settlers. Roger Williams, the founder of Rhode Island, wrote: "I feared the distractions of the games, and would not attend them in order that I might not countenance and partake of their folly after I saw the evil of them."

The families, relatives and friends formed cheering squads along the sidelines. The women and girls would dance and sing, while the boys accompanied them by blowing on hollow reeds and beating sticks together. If the teams were of equal strength, it might take two or three days to determine a winner. Afterward, however, everyone sat down to a bountiful meal and vibrant merrymaking before returning home.

The Indians loved to gamble on the outcome of the games. The betting was conducted in an organized manner, and usually was overseen by the more influential and older men of the tribe. Often an Indian would wager everything that he owned on the outcome of a single game, risking his clothes, food, knives, wampum and even his tribal standing.

From these roots, soccer grew into a favorite sport of the early American settlers.

• • •

Football became part of the English school system in 1580, when Cambridge made it part of its intramural program. It was first played on an intercollegiate basis in 1620, and continued to develop in the public and private schools and universities in England, as well as the colleges and preparatory schools of the United States.

The game remained a rough, often violent sport, however, into the 1800s as it lacked organization and a specific set of rules. The field of play still was as long as 200 yards in some locations and each town or school seemed to have its unique set of rules, although players were not allowed to run with the ball.

A landmark event occurred in 1823, when William Webb Ellis, a student at a public school named Rugby (in England, public schools are the equivalent of American private schools, and vice-versa) showed blatant disregard for the rules and picked up the ball and ran with it during a game. Ellis' rebellious display was not popular with his fellow students or teachers at the rigidly governed school, but he now is considered the father of rugby and American football. A field at Rugby contains a historical marker noting his "contribution."

This incident led to a controversy over whether players should be allowed to carry the ball, and the game's followers split into divisions: the "carriers" (rugby players) and "dribblers" (soccer players). Other differences of opinion regarding offside, throw-ins, kicking below the legs and the number of players permitted on a team added to the division.

Finally, in 1848 at Trinity College in Cambridge, representatives from several universities gathered to write the first set of rules. These rules forbid pushing, tripping, holding, or touching the ball with the hands except to catch it or knock it down so that it could be kicked, and therefore alienated the rugby followers. The separate factions intensified. An attempt to formulate a more formal code was made in 1862 by J.C. Thring, who wrote rules for use in the matches at Cambridge. He called his version of football "The Simplest Game," and published 10 basic, conservative rules that furthered the cause of the football "dribblers."

The disagreement ultimately resulted in a formal split that gave birth to both sports. The Football Association was formed in October of 1863, during a meeting at the Freemason's Tavern in London. Representatives of 11 clubs met one evening to begin formulating official rules, from which the modern soccer code evolved. This is generally considered the birthdate of soccer, as the game is played today. An association that gave birth to rugby was formed in later years.

Most of the rules were general in nature, such as the mandates that the field be no more than 200 yards long and goal posts be no more than eight yards apart. Two rules, however, fueled the controversy between the two factions. Carrying or running with the ball was forbidden, as was "hacking," kicking an opponent in the shins to stop his progress with the ball.

One club, the Blackheath Football Club of London, believed hacking was an integral part of what they considered to be a man's game. They and others who agreed with them left the Football Association and continued with their rougher version of the game. Hacking, however, soon became unpopular among rugby followers, and was disallowed as a defensive tactic late in the 1860s.

It was about this time that the word "soccer" was coined. To understand how it happened, you have to know two things. One, rugby was often called "rugger" in those days. Two, Association was often abbreviated as "Assoc." Legend has it that Charles Wreford-Brown, a student at Oxford, told a friend one day that he was going out to play "soccer" instead of "rugger," and the name stuck.

• • •

The game that would become soccer was the most popular sport in the American schools for much of the 19th century. Princeton students played a soccer-like game as far back as 1820. Harvard students played another crude version of the game starting in 1827. The freshman and sophomore classes met each fall on the first day of classes for an annual game that became known as "Bloody Monday" because of its violence. Harvard authorities eventually banned the game, but the students continued to play it in less formal fashion.

The first organized nonscholastic soccer club in the United States was the Oneida Football Club of Boston. It was formed in the summer of 1862 and lasted three seasons, during which it was undefeated and unscored upon.

The club was assembled by Gerrit Smith Miller, who was a pupil at the Epes Sargent Dixwell Private Latin School of Boston. Twelve players were drafted from the Dixwell School, two from Boston English High School and one from the Boston Public Latin School. The team played by rules very similar to the code that was adopted by the Football Association in England in 1863.

James D'Wolf Lovett, a player on the Oneida Club, wrote in his memoirs, *Old Boston Boys and the Games They Played,* that, "It was a very strong club and played matches repeatedly with the Public Latin School, English High School and

Dorchester High School, beating them so easily that a match was made with the combined forces of the Boston Latin and English High schools. Even this array could make no headway against us."

The Boston Society for the Preservation of New England Antiquities in 1923 was presented with the ball — a round object with a rubberized canvas cover — that was used for Oneida's game against the combined team. The society also received the uniform worn by the players, a simple but distinctive red handkerchief that was tied around the head, Indian style.

In Boston on the Common near the Spruce Street Gate, a six-foot, six-inch high monument was erected on November 21st, 1925 to commemorate the Oneida Club as the first organized football team in America. It read:

> "ON THIS FIELD THE ONEIDA FOOTBALL CLUB OF BOSTON, THE FIRST ORGANIZED FOOTBALL CLUB IN THE UNITED STATES, PLAYED AGAINST ALL COMERS FROM 1862 TO 1865. THE ONEIDA GOAL WAS NEVER CROSSED."

Organized team sports came of age in the United States following the end of the Civil War. At first, such activities were a pastime for men from wealthy families, who were the only ones with enough free time to participate. The post-war years of the 1870s and 1880s brought a new wave of immigrants to America, however, most of whom settled in the eastern half of the United States where the Industrial Revolution provided jobs. By the 1880s, advancing labor legislation was beginning to provide more leisure time for the working class.

Employers in these places encouraged their foreign-born employees to participate in soccer as an inducement to remain in the small industrial towns and villages. For the first time, the common man of limited means was acquiring an interest in recreation and team sports were losing their status as the preserve of the student or man of wealth.

Soccer continued to gain in popularity in the universities, particularly in the eastern part of the country, as an intramural sport. The first intercollegiate game in the United States was played between Princeton and Rutgers in 1869; Rutgers won, 6-4. During the next two decades, many colleges throughout the eastern United States began fielding teams. Rugby was becoming more popular too, however, and the two sports appeared locked on a collision course.

An attempt was made to organize a soccer league among eastern colleges at a meeting on October 19, 1873. It could have been the historical equivalent of the Football Association meeting at the Freemason's Tavern in England if not for Harvard's refusal to participate. Princeton, Rutgers, Yale and Columbia agreed to form the Intercollegiate Football Association, but Harvard chose to throw its considerable influence behind rugby.

Harvard's decision was a major blow to U.S. soccer. Rugby football became America's primary fall attraction, while association football, or soccer, became a "minor" sport.

Some historians view this moment as a major turning point in the history of soccer. If Harvard had thrown its considerable weight behind soccer instead of rugby, they believe, soccer would have become the dominant collegiate game in the United States rather than our modern version of football, which evolved from rugby.

Others disagree, noting that the rules changes that altered rugby probably would have defaced soccer as well, leaving an unimaginable hybrid sport. Perhaps it was just as well, they believe, that soccer was left behind to grow on its own at a slower pace.

The Intercollegiate Football Association, which governed rugby in the U.S., was formed in 1876. A group to govern U.S. soccer, the American Football Association, was not formed until 1884, by which time the abundance of immigration from Britain and Ireland had accelerated the growth of soccer and brought about the need for such an organization. Until the AFA was formed, the administration of soccer was split among several regional groups with various interpretations of the rules to suit local tastes.

The AFA organized the first international competition for U.S. teams. The first game against an opponent from outside the country was in November of 1885 against the Canadian national team in East Newark, New Jersey. A team of standout players from the New Jersey area represented the U.S. Most of the players on both teams were immigrants from England and Scotland who had played the game in their native countries. The Canadians won 1-0 before about 2,000 fans. A report in The New York *Times* noted that the game was interrupted by numerous fist fights. The Canadian team went on to win three more games against local teams before returning home.

The U.S. won its first game ever in international competition the following November against the Canadians in Kearny, New Jersey. Another crowd of about 2,000 spectators watched a group of local standouts win 3-2 on a rainy, windy afternoon.

The AFA helped the growth of soccer until 1899, when a series of circumstances brought its activities to a halt. Thousands of laborers had lost their jobs early in the decade, and the resulting depression made it impossible for the New England industrial clubs to function. And in New York, New Jersey and Pennsylvania, professionalism was creating havoc among the amateur clubs and their players. The ruthless tactics of many teams in acquiring players ruined the plans for an orderly and efficient operation.

George Morehouse, left, of the New York Americans and Alec McNabb, right, of the St. Louis Bombers participate in a coin toss with legendary referee Jimmy Walder. Walder's career spanned seven decades. He refereed his first match in 1909 and his last in 1969 at the age of 84.

 **2**

The 20th Century

Professional games officially began in England in 1888 with the organization of the Football League, which was the brainchild of a Scot named William McGregor. Some teams had been paying players illegally, but the decision of the Football Association in 1885 to recognize the professional element and allow pro teams to compete for the F.A. Cup opened the door to a professional league venture. It was an historic moment for the sport, and it helped elevate professional soccer to a stable and respected position in the athletic world.

The Football League was composed of 12 teams. It remained unchanged until 1962, when one of the teams, Accrington, had to fold because of a lack of funds. A point system of awarding two points for a victory and one for a tie also was initiated. This system still is used today all over the world except in some of the American professional leagues.

The amateurs were as good as, or better than, the professionals at first, but by 1900 the pros were dominating. The formation of professional leagues brought added emphasis to the game, with more time devoted to training and strategy, and raised it to a higher level. As the games improved, attendance increased. In 1901, 110,000 fans filled the Crystal Palace stadium in England for the Football Association Cup final.

The sudden surge in popularity propelled the game around the world, as British sailors, soldiers, engineers, businessmen and educators introduced it during their travels. It was met with enthusiasm throughout Europe, Russia and South America. British businessmen introduced the game in Denmark. Two brothers who owned a cotton mill in Russia introduced the game there. Miners took the game to Spain and Rumania. The British Embassy staff taught it in Sweden. Sailors showed it to the people of Brazil. Educators taught the game in Argentina and Uruguay. English gardeners introduced it in Austria.

As more and more football associations were formed in distant places in the world — 16 had been formed by 1900 — the need arose for an international governing body. The Football Association in England had no interest in taking on the task, so in May of 1904 the Federation Internationale de Football Association (FIFA) was founded by representatives from Belgium, Denmark, France, Holland, Spain, Sweden, and Switzerland.

FIFA remains the international governing body today, with more than 140 members. It controls the game's rules, and coordinates the competition for the World Cup and the Olympics. It also sets standards for officiating, determines whether players should be classified as amateurs or professionals, and disciplines players, teams and national organizations.

• • •

Professional soccer officially came to the United States in 1894 when the American League of Professional Football (Soccer) Clubs was formed along the Eastern seaboard.

The league was founded by the six owners of teams in the Eastern Division of the National Baseball League. They were hoping the venture would keep their stadiums occupied and bring in more money after the baseball season ended. Each team was to play a 50-game schedule, with four games a week, from Oct. 1 to Jan. 1.

The league faced trouble before it even began play, however. The AFA, resenting the invasion of the baseball owners into soccer and feeling threatened by the fact they were signing amateur players to professional contracts, issued a warning that no player could play for an AFA team if he signed a professional contract. This was unlike the situation in England, where the amateurs and pros both played under the authority of the Football Association, adhering to uniform rules and regulations.

Still, the baseball owners pressed onward. They were hopeful that the soccer fans in the eastern cities would immediately support the new league and create a nucleus upon which to build enthusiasm for the game. Newspapers provided widespread coverage, explaining the game to readers who had not yet seen it.

Managers of the professional baseball teams were hired to coach the soccer teams, too, although they had little or no knowledge of the game. Only Baltimore was directed by a true soccer coach. Its general manager, Ned Hanlon, sought an advantage over the other league members by importing a professional coach from

England, A. W. Stewart. Through his overseas connections, Stewart was able to sign eight prominent English professional players.

The other teams hired some of the professionals who had come to the United States to play for industrial soccer clubs; many professional players from Scotland, England and Ireland found that they could make more money playing soccer in the United States because no salary limits were imposed. Amateur players were hired, too.

The American League of Professional Football Clubs began play on October 6, 1894. Its teams included the Boston Beaneaters, the New York Giants, the Washington Senators, the Baltimore Orioles, the Philadelphia Quakers and the Brooklyn Superbas. The admission charge was 25 cents, financially within reach of the ordinary working man.

On opening day, Boston defeated Brooklyn 3-2 at the South End Grounds in Boston while in New York City the Giants defeated Philadelphia 5-0 at the Polo Grounds. The new soccer venture of the baseball professionals was received enthusiastically by Washington *Post*, which reported:

"Reports from Philadelphia and Boston indicate that the new game will be a big success. The playing of the four teams was of a character to stir up lots of enthusiasm and excitement."

Twelve days later, however, on October 18th, Boston defeated New York 4-3 at the Polo Grounds in New York before a slim gathering of fewer than 100 fans. This was a typical crowd for a weekday game, when most of the soccer fans were working.

The promoters had failed to realize that most of the support for the league would come from the foreign-born blue collar workers of the eastern industrial states. The ordinary wage earner was available only on Saturdays and Sundays. They also failed to coordinate the opening of the soccer season with the conclusion of the National Baseball League playoffs, a blunder that made their new venture that much easier to ignore.

Baltimore's opening game was delayed because of the baseball playoffs, but the Orioles turned out to be the most talented and popular team in the league. They won their opening game over Washington 5-1 and received considerable space in the Baltimore *Sun*, which reported:

> "A crowd estimated to contain 8,000 persons saw yesterday the first professional football game ever played in Baltimore. The team defeated Washington 5-1 and the spectators rooted with delight when they observed the extraordinary skill employed by the players. The game was no less a startling surprise than a pleasant novelty. The spectators had never dreamed of the opportunities for brilliant scientific play, for the strategy and for quickly executed movements of mind and body."

The league's troubles reached a peak after Baltimore defeated Washington 10-1 in Washington on Oct. 16. A story in The Washington *Post* the next day reported:

> "Baltimore's professional football team found Washington about as easy to beat as the baseball Orioles found the Senators during the baseball season. Manager Ned Hanlon never does things by halves so when he went into football he worked with the same energy that characterized his work in baseball.

> "To use a sporting phrase, Hanlon 'rung in a cold deck' on the other managers of the league."

As a result of the uproar over the game, Immigration Department officials of the United States Treasury Department were asked to investigate whether or not the federal labor laws pertaining to alien workers could be applied to professional sports activities.

The confrontation between the immigration authorities and officials of the Baltimore club, who claimed nearly all of their players were from Detroit, left a cloud hanging over the entire league. Although the newspapers credited the Baltimore players with being former champions of England, the team actually had been a new addition to the English League Second Division. The players in question had jumped their contracts with the newly formed English team. All the men involved were top-class professionals, and their defection had created a small sensation in the British newspapers.

PHOTO COURTESY NATIONAL SOCCER HALL OF FAME

The Oakland Hornets of 1904-05, one of the earliest West Coast teams.

Action in a Boston District League game 1908. The referee is at left, wearing black.

Ultimately, all of this did not matter. As league play continued, the league directors had secretly met in New York City on Oct. 19 and decided to close down the league before it was three weeks old.

The league failed largely because the owners had not fully researched their idea, and had done little to promote the sport to prospective fans. The league could have changed the destiny of soccer in the United States, but professional soccer would have to wait. The final standing of the clubs listed Baltimore in first place with a 6-0 record.

The league's failure had a distressing effect on others who might have been tempted to promote the professional game. Plans were being made for a professional league made up of the better clubs in the American Football (Soccer) Association in the late 1890s, but the Spanish-American War of 1898 and the general labor unrest in New England and other mill districts prevented it from happening.

In fact, the war and labor strife had a depressing effect on the entire soccer scene and slowed the progress of the American Football Association. The American Cup competition, emblematic of the national soccer championship, was abandoned from 1899 to 1906.

• • •

Interest in soccer was waning in the United States during the first decade of the 20th century, but the appearance of two touring all-star teams from England helped spark a resurgence. An English team, the Pilgrim F.C., toured Canada and the United States in 1905. Another English team, the Corinthians, toured in 1906. These trips drew favorable coverage from the newspapers and brought out many fans.

Soccer again became part of the sports curriculum in American schools and colleges in 1905, after being relatively dormant for several years. Hope was renewed that soccer would be nurtured into a popular collegiate sport to complement the growth of the game in amateur circles, particularly after President Theodore Roosevelt threatened to eliminate American football as a college pastime unless the violence was controlled.

Soccer still did not catch on as hoped, but support was mustered for the formation of an Intercollegiate Soccer League for the 1906 season, with Columbia, Cornell, Harvard, Haverford and Pennsylvania competing. The league lasted until 1925, when the Intercollegiate Soccer Association was formed in its place. During the depression years of the 1930s, regional leagues were developed in the Middle Atlantic states and in New England.

The American Football Association regrouped in 1906. Originally an organization for amateur teams, it began looking out for professional teams as well. The AFA focused its interest in the East, however, displaying little interest in national expansion. This led to a growing feeling among rival soccer groups that a more progressive administration was needed to govern the sport. As a result, the American Amateur Football (Soccer) Association was formed.

Thomas Cahill, an American-born sports executive from St. Louis, who was secretary of the New York State Association, and Thomas Bagnall, President of the New York group, set up the federation to command allegiance from the national and international elements of the game. Dr. G. Randolph Manning of New York was elected to the presidency of the AAFA at its general meeting in New York City on September 5, 1912, and Cahill was elected secretary.

Dr. Manning had been born in England, but pursued his medical studies in Germany, where he played soccer and became involved in the administrative affairs of German soccer. He helped form the German Football Association in 1904, and helped obtain FIFA recognition for it. Later he moved to the United States to practice medicine in New York City.

With international soccer in his background, Dr. Manning soon advocated membership in FIFA. He sent Cahill to the Ninth Annual Congress of FIFA at Stockholm, Sweden on June 30 and July 1, 1912, during the Olympic Games, for the purpose of gaining membership in the international body.

The American Football Association was seeking an affiliation of its own with FIFA, and was unaware of Cahill's presence at the congress until advised by its British contacts. Fearing that it would lose out to the rival American Amateur Football Association, it requested F. J. Wall, secretary of the Football Association of England, to present its case.

Cahill put forth a proposal on behalf of the American Amateur Football Association, but it was opposed by Wall, who based his objections on the fact that the American Amateur Football Association did not control both the professional and amateur groups in the United States. He suggested to FIFA that Cahill be advised to return to America and help bring the warring factions into a single union. FIFA agreed, saying it would accept an American affiliate after the dispute was resolved.

The rebuff by FIFA did not deter Cahill and his associates. Upon his return to the United States, Cahill and two associates, William Campbell and N. Ager, met with a similar committee from the American Football Association. Negotiations for a common front appeared to be progressing favorably, but on December 8, 1912 the American Football Association announced that its "peace" committee had been discharged. This setback brought a halt to the plans for a merger of the two associations.

Dr. Manning and Cahill decided to seek the cooperation of the Allied American Football Association of Philadelphia, a large and well-governed body not yet committed to either side, to create a truly national federation. At a private meeting in New York City on March 8, 1913, the Allied American representatives agreed to assist the American Amateur Football Association in the formation of a national organization.

Soccer-minded people from across the nation met at the Astor House in New York City on April 5 for the first national soccer convention in the United States. From this session came the name of a new organization, the United States Football Association. On June 21, the by-laws and rules of procedure were passed and a set of officers was elected, with Dr. Manning as president.

After the April 5 meeting, a new application for recognition was forwarded to FIFA on behalf of the new United States of America Football Association. The official formation of the USFA was not completed until after the FIFA meeting in Copenhagen, so the application was turned over to the Emergency Committee with instructions to recognize the group after a permanent organization had been set up.

Speculation continued regarding which group — the USFA or the AFA — would be accepted by FIFA. Finally, on August 15, 1913, a cablegram from Europe advised the United States Football Association that it had been granted provisional mem-

The Bethlehem Football Club, sponsored by Bethlehem Steel, was the best team in the country during the century's second decade. Here the team poses before defeating Brooklyn for the United States Football Association championship in May of 1915.

bership. The next day the American Football Association decided by a 10-2 vote to submit to the authority of the new national association. The soccer organizers had ended their long power struggle. Permanent membership was granted on June 21, 1914.

• • •

It was about this time that professional soccer in the United States began to flourish after several false starts. In 1901, plans had been made to create a professional soccer league in the Midwest with teams from St. Louis, Chicago, Detroit and Milwaukee. Charles Comiskey, owner of the Chicago White Sox baseball team, and other major league owners from midwestern cities expressed interest, but the financial support never materialized. Semi-professional regional leagues were formed and had some success, but none of the players were full-time professionals.

In 1909, representatives from the major soccer centers of the East met to form a new professional league, the Eastern League, in Newark, N.J. Six teams joined, including two from Philadelphia. The league barely survived one season, discontinuing play after an abbreviated schedule. Although the games drew well, inclement weather caused insurmountable scheduling difficulties that led to an early demise.

The Eastern League was succeeded by the National League, which would last until 1921. The National League was hardly national in scope, however. To keep traveling expenses low, it restricted its teams to the states of New York, New Jersey and Pennsylvania.

The first great American professional soccer team, the Bethlehem Steel F.C., emerged in Bethlehem, Pennsylvania during the second decade of the 20th century. The team's success was assured because the upper management of the steel company took a serious interest in the team, recruiting the best professional talent available from the U.S. and overseas, giving them jobs with the steel company and paying them a bonus for playing soccer. Some of them did not have to work for the company at all, and concentrated solely on playing soccer.

In an era when professional baseball and collegiate football were the most popular team sports, the team drew a wide following. It won the National Challenge Cup, which was in effect the national championship, in the 1914-15 and 1915-16 seasons. It also won the American Challenge Cup, a similar competition that was soon disbanded, in 1915-16, the only soccer team to win a "double" national championship.

Bethlehem's opponent in the championship game of the 1916 National Challenge Cup was Fall River, an intense rival because of the proximity and quality of the two teams. Bethlehem won 1-0 before 10,000 fans at Pawtucket in a game that was marred by a major brawl involving players and spectators at the end of the game.

PHOTO COURTESY PAUL HARRIS

The famous Bethlehem Steel team later participated in the original American Soccer League in 1921 as the Philadelphia entry.

George Young in a photograph taken sometime in the 1920s. Young, a Scotsman, was one of the game's pioneer referees. Note his clothing and shoes. Nets were not commonly attached to the goals until the 1960s, but were in use here.

PHOTO COURTESY PAUL HARRIS

Noted soccer referee James Walder makes a presentation after the Junior Cup championship of the United States Soccer Federation in 1928.

• • •

Although World War I, which lasted from 1914 to 1918, had a depressing effect on American soccer, as it did on the whole of American life, the end of hostilities released another wave of immigrants to the United States. By the early 1920s the time was right for another attempt to organize a major professional soccer league.

The 1920s are known as the "Golden Age of Sport" because athletic competition became a more popular attraction than ever before and athletes such as Red Grange, Babe Ruth and Jack Dempsey became national heroes.

The American Soccer League — a full-time league in which the players had no other jobs — was formed amid this booming period in 1921, with eight teams in five eastern states. The ASL began play in the fall of 1921 and remained an eight-team league until the 1924-1925 season, although several franchises changed hands during that time. Four more teams were added to the league that season, boosting the membership to 12 teams.

The decade turned out to be a golden age for soccer, too, as many of the best players in the world joined ASL teams. The league, which played on Saturdays, Sundays and holidays, was helped by the fact the British had angrily withdrawn from FIFA in 1920 because of Germany's membership in the organization — the result of lingering bitterness over World War I — and did not rejoin until 1924. During this time, many prominent players from the British Isles joined ASL teams, as did other skilled players from Europe.

ASL teams attracted between 5,000 and 10,000 fans per game on the average, and as many as 20,000 for big games. Writeups on individual players and teams appeared in the sports pages of the larger metropolitan daily newspapers for the first time, making them more popular than ever to the masses. This period was called the "Renaissance of American Soccer." A sportswriter of the time said, "We really didn't think too much about European soccer then. The best soccer being played anywhere was right here in America."

Cahill was the primary force behind the ASL, just as he had helped form the American Amateur Football Association and the United States Football Association. Cahill's dream was to make soccer as popular in the United States as it was in other parts of the world, and to establish it as the national pastime for the fall, winter and spring months.

At the same time the ASL was getting started, a league of professional football teams, who played the American version of the game that would grow into the National Football League we know today, was getting underway with teams in many of the same cities as the ASL. Together, the ASL and NFL were invading the professional sports arena that had been the private sanctuary of baseball for many years. Meanwhile, to accommodate the needs of the amateurs, the United States Football Association instituted the National Amateur Cup competition in 1923.

The strength of American soccer during this period was reflected by the success some of the teams had against touring foreign teams. In 1926, the powerful Hakoah team from Vienna toured the eastern U.S. and drew record crowds: 25,000, 30,000 and 36,000 fans in successive games. Still, the trip wasn't a success for the visitors. It lost games and lost money, more than $30,000.

During the spring of 1927, the Uruguayan national team, which had won the 1924 Olympics and would later win the 1928 Olympics and 1930 World Cup, toured the U.S. and was defeated by the Newark All-Stars — its first loss in three years.

• • •

Despite the game's growth during this period, dissatisfaction was simmering between the amateur and professional factions of the United States Football Association. The ASL at this time was governed by Commissioner Bill Cunningham, a national sports columnist from the Boston *Morning Post.* Cunningham, originally from Texas, had been an All-American football player at Dartmouth College and was a respected influence in professional and intercollegiate football. He was hired in an attempt to secure additional recognition for the ASL from the news media. Although this move had some merit, it was unfortunate that a man more familiar with soccer and its nuances was not at the helm during this difficult period for the game.

Trouble mounted at the Helsinki Congress of FIFA in 1927 when the USFA was threatened with expulsion for harboring and playing foreign professional players who had jumped their contracts overseas. It was only through the diplomacy of Andrew M. Brown, the USFA president, that the threat was averted.

Another major problem arose over the National Challenge Cup competition. The management of the ASL did not want its teams to compete for the Cup because the competition interfered with the league schedule. When the New York Giants, Bethlehem Steel and Newark defied the league order and entered the national competition, they were suspended by the ASL. The USFA failed to recognize the ASL's decision, however, and refused to declare the clubs ineligible.

The suspended teams remained in good standing with the United States Football Association and organized a new professional league, the Eastern League. Bethlehem Steel, Newark, the New York Giants, New York Hispano, New York Hungaria, New York Hakoah, I.R.T. Rangers and the Newark Portuguese became members of the new group.

The American Soccer League and the Eastern League began a struggle for the support of the soccer populace to their mutual disadvantage until Cahill, secretary of the USFA, negotiated a peace settlement on October 9, 1929. The wounds of the battle were felt for many years, however. Many influential and wealthy men, such as H.E. Lewis of Bethlehem Steel and G.A.G. Wood of American Woolen Company, became disillusioned with the soccer situation and withdrew from the game.

The dissension and the economic depression of the 1930s brought an end to an era in which the United States seemed to be emerging as a major world soccer power. Not until the past few years has it regrouped to the point where it stands in a similar position.

PHOTO COURTESY PROF. JULIO MAZZEI

Pelé is the most famous player in the history of soccer. He led Brazil to three World Cup championships and later came out of retirement to play for the New York Cosmos of the North American Soccer League from 1975-77. As a player and ambassador of the game, he introduced soccer to the masses in the United States and spawned a legion of young players known as the "Pelé Generation."

 **3**

The Modern Game

The history of modern professional soccer in the United States has been spotty, filled with highlights and low moments. Several leagues have come and gone, but the sport appears to be on solid footing in both its outdoor and indoor versions entering the 1990s.

A new American Soccer League, completely divorced from the old group, was organized for the 1933-1934 season. The old league had been a pretentious effort to promote American professional soccer on a major scale with elite professional players. The re-created ASL, in a Depression-ridden world, was reluctant to expand beyond the narrow corridor between New York City and Baltimore.

The ASL survived the Depression, made it through World War II, and lasted until 1982 with varying degrees of success. Its most successful ventures were exhibition games it arranged with visiting professional teams. Starting in 1946, the league by itself or in conjunction with the United States Football Association financed visits from teams from all over the world. In return, American Soccer League teams visited Mexico, Cuba, Israel and Central and South America.

Apart from the commercial aspects of the tours, they had a very positive effect on the progress of soccer in the United States. American players benefitted from playing against the foreign teams and the soccer public was able to watch the best talent from all parts of the world.

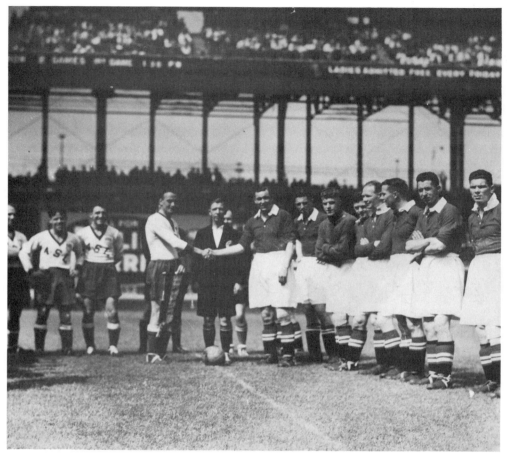

An all-star team from the American Soccer League met a touring team from England at the Polo Grounds in New York City in 1937. More than 23,000 fans attended the game.

Meanwhile, a sports promoter and entrepreneur named Bill Cox formed the International Soccer League in 1960. Cox's plan was to import foreign teams from South America and Europe, intact, and have them play in the United States during their off-seasons. The ISL became an immediate success, and was endorsed by FIFA and the United States Soccer Federation. It expanded to both coasts and drew well, but folded in 1964 after becoming immersed in political squabbling with FIFA and the United States Soccer Federation.

An event that gave major impetus to professional soccer in the U.S. — to soccer in general, for that matter — was the 1966 World Cup final between England and West Germany in London. England's 4-2 victory, played before 100,000 fans, drew high television ratings and motivated a great number of businessmen to start franchises.

The United States Soccer Federation and the Canadian Soccer Football Association received so many applications for franchises that two leagues were formed. FIFA, however, would recognize only one league from each country. An attempt was made to merge the teams into one league before they began play, but it failed.

The two leagues — the United Soccer Association and the National Professional Soccer League — began play in 1967. The United Soccer Association gained the official recognition of the governing bodies, but the NPSL had a television contract from CBS that proved to be almost as valuable. The USA attracted better players by importing entire teams from foreign countries, but the NPSL received more exposure.

Most of the teams in both leagues lost money that first season, however. Motivated by self-preservation and FIFA's urgings, the two leagues merged into the North American Soccer League in December of 1967 with 17 teams — eight from the USA, seven from the NPSL and two new ones.

The vast majority of the players came from outside of the United States and Canada. Communication between coaches and players was often difficult because of language barriers, and the startup league ran into many financial and administrative problems. Twelve franchises folded after the first season in 1968, leaving just five to play the following year. A playoff format obviously wasn't suitable for five teams, so the league champion that season was determined by points.

The league rebounded the following year after Phil Woosnam and Clive Toye were brought in as executives. It lost one member, but picked up two teams from the ASL to grow to six, and attendance increased. The league grew slowly but steadily through the 1970s. It received a boost in 1973 when Kyle Rote Jr., a member of the Dallas team, was named rookie of the year, a landmark event in a league still dominated by foreign players. Rote's popularity, which was enhanced by his victories in nationally televised athletic competition against professional athletes from other sports, was crucial to the league's growth.

The following season, 1974, brought several breakthroughs. Six new franchises joined the league, including four on the west coast. The league had truly become a national league. League attendance surpassed one million that year, and the championship game between Los Angeles and Miami was televised. A tiebreaking system was introduced as well, in which penalty kicks were used to settle deadlocked scores. Los Angeles won its championship by hitting all five of its penalty shots, while Miami made just four.

The ASL, meanwhile, was making changes as well. It had struggled through the 1970 and '71 seasons with just five teams, but expanded in following years to become more national in scope. In an effort to attract more attention from the national sports media and to open new avenues to investors, the league hired Bob Cousy, a Hall of Fame basketball great with the Boston Celtics, as its Commissioner in 1974. It was reminiscent of 1926, when the "original" American Soccer League appointed Bill Cunningham, the nationally syndicated sports writer and former All- American football player, as Commissioner.

Although Cousy's appointment was greeted with skepticism among soccer followers, the ASL did continue to grow under Cousy's leadership, reaching the West Coast in 1976. Still, it operated in the shadows of the NASL, largely because of a bold move by Toye, then a Cosmos executive.

Toye, backed by wealthy ownership, signed Pelé to a $4.5 million contract in 1975, convincing the retired legend that only he could establish soccer in the United States. The money didn't hurt, either. Pelé already had played in 65 countries and scored more than 1,100 goals in nearly 20 years of play, but now he was starting over with a new mission.

The signing of Pelé started a trend, as other retired or over-the-hill foreign stars were signed to league contracts. It was Pelé, however, who was most responsible for bringing in new fans. He was a charismatic and tireless ambassador who introduced the game to many Americans.

Pelé couldn't lead the Cosmos to the league championship his first two years, however. He then announced the 1977 season would be his last. Toye, intent on making Pelé's last season a championship season, signed Franz Beckenbauer, captain of the West German team and perhaps the best player in the world at the time, to a contract. With former Italian star Giorgio Chinaglia already on hand, the Cosmos had three of the world's great players, although not necessarily in their prime.

The Cosmos won the championship that year and averaged about 35,000 fans per game. The peak moment came on August 14, 1977 at Giants Stadium in the Meadowlands of New Jersey when a capacity crowd of 77,691 watched Pelé and the New York Cosmos defeat the Ft. Lauderdale Strikers, 8-3, in a playoff game. It was the largest crowd ever to watch a soccer game in the United States.

Less than 60 days later, a game in the same stadium marked the final international tribute to Pelé. Honoring his retirement as a player, 72,000 attended a game on October 1, 1977 between the only two teams he had been associated with as a player, Santos of Brazil and the Cosmos. Played in the pouring rain, the game ended in a 2-1 victory for the American club. Pelé played half the game for each team, scoring a first-half goal for the Cosmos. Known as Pelé to the world, Edson to his friends, and Dico to his family, this one man had brought to light what lesser men had not accomplished in decades of hard work: acceptance of the game among Americans.

At that final game, hundreds of young players surrounded the field in tribute to their hero. The public address announcer proclaimed the young players as the "Pelé Generation," a valid indication of his impact.

Unfortunately for the NASL, things returned to "normal" after Pelé's retirement. Although many new fans had been introduced to the league, it did not draw nearly as well without him. The ASL continued to struggle, too, as it became evident there wasn't enough support for the game to support two leagues.

The ASL folded in 1982. The NASL hung on for two more seasons, folding in March of 1985 before the start of that year's season. It was a major blow to soccer fans in the United States, but almost as quickly as that league died new seeds were planted. The Western Soccer Alliance, later renamed the Western Soccer League, was formed in July of 1985 with four teams, and still another version of the American Soccer League began play in 1988 on the East Coast.

As before, the realities of fan interest and expenses soon made it clear that two leagues could not survive simultaneously. On Feb. 22, 1990, they merged into the American Professional Soccer League for business and marketing purposes, but continued to play in separate conferences without interleague play.

The following season the league truly became one, with a national schedule and official recognition from the United States Soccer Federation. The San Francisco Bay and Albany teams, both runners-up in their conferences, met for the championship, which San Francisco won. The final game was played before 12,411 fans and a national cable television audience.

• • •

Indoor soccer was introduced at Madison Square Garden in New York City in the winter of 1939, and has been played off and on in various parts of the country since then. Although the field dimensions and rules vary somewhat from the outdoor game, indoor soccer, with its dasher boards and faster surface, has attracted a solid core of fans who enjoy the fast- paced, less structured form. It is somewhat a cross between outdoor soccer and ice hockey.

The spark for the first indoor professional league came in the winter of 1974 when the Philadelphia Atoms of the NASL played a Soviet team in the Philadelphia Spectrum before 13,000 fans.

Three years later, on Nov. 10, 1977, 12 businessmen met in New York City to form the Major Indoor Soccer League. The league started play in 1978-79 with six teams, and expanded to as many as 12 in the 1980s. It changed its name to the Major Soccer League in the summer of 1990. It had nine teams as of 1992.

Another indoor league, the National Professional Soccer League, has operated since 1984. Originally named the American Indoor Soccer Association, it has fluctuated between four and nine teams, and had nine as of 1992.

The two indoor leagues take sharply different approaches to the game. The NPSL, for example, has a multiple scoring system similar to basketball, with goals counting between one and three points. It also uses a larger goal and has adjusted the rules to encourage a faster-paced game. The NPSL stipulates that all of its players must be American citizens or green card holders (no more than two per team), while the MSL allows the use of foreign players.

• • •

Soccer has been played formally or informally in the schools of the United States since the 1860s. Only since the turn of the century, however, has the game actually made consistent inroads into the athletic programs of the public schools.

New York City was the first municipality to include soccer as a part of the athletic curriculum, doing so in the fall of 1905. The school authorities in such cities as Boston, Philadelphia, Baltimore, Newark, and other cities in the East had introduced soccer into their elementary schools by 1920, and in some cases had extended the game into their high school activities. In St. Louis in the Midwest and in San Francisco, Los Angeles and Salt Lake City in the West, the sport was played in some of the elementary grades on an intramural basis.

High schools, influenced by the professional and college football element, were reluctant to accept soccer as a varsity sport, but in the elementary schools it was viewed as an acceptable physical activity. In New York, Pennsylvania, New Jersey, Maryland, Delaware, Massachusetts, Connecticut, Rhode Island and New Hampshire, some private preparatory and public high schools were participating in soccer before World War 1.

During the 1920s and 1930s, high school soccer began to receive grudging acceptance from enlightened school administrators, continuing to have its main roots in the East. An occasional team or league was found in the Midwest or on the Pacific Coast.

Beginning in 1946, secondary school soccer began the growth which continues today. In 1971, 1,768 high schools in 24 states included soccer in their athletic programs. By 1977, soccer was a major sport in more than 4,000 high schools. In 1987 the number of schools offering soccer to boys and girls exceeded 10,000, and in 1991 the number exceeded 13,000.

The sport has grown similarly on the collegiate level. At the end of 1946, 86 U.S. colleges were playing the sport. In 1991, more than 800 schools fielded men's teams and another 600 had women's programs.

The formation of the National Soccer Coaches Association in 1941 was a landmark event for American collegiate soccer. It provided a forum for ideas from coaches from all regions of the United States, and created a working organization for a concerted effort. Many innovations were sponsored for college soccer by the coaches group.

On December 14, 1946, the first all-star collegiate game was played at Sterling Oval in New York City, as a South team defeated a North team, 1- 0. At Sportsmen's Park in St. Louis on New Year's Day 1950, more than 5,000 spectators watched Penn State and San Francisco tie, 1-1, in the first Soccer Bowl game.

The National Collegiate Athletic Association (NCAA) conducted the first official championship in 1959. St. Louis, coached by the legendary Bob Guelker, defeated Bridgeport in the final game, 5-2, the first of nine championships it would win over the next 15 years. Guelker coached the team until 1966, winning five NCAA titles. His successor, Harry Keough, won four, finished second once, and had one final game appearance, against Michigan State in 1967, cancelled because of bad weather.

Championships for Division II and Division III schools were introduced in 1972 and 1974, respectively.

A women's Division I championship was inaugurated in 1982. North Carolina won all but one of the championships played from then until 1991. Division II and Division III championships were added for women later in the 1980s. The National Association for Intercollegiate Athletics (NAIA) began a championship for its men's teams in 1959 and added a tournament for the women's teams in 1981.

• • •

Oscar Wilde once said, "Soccer may be perfectly all right for tough girls, but not the right sport for gentle lads."

All over the United States, "tough" girls are playing the sport in increasing numbers. Nearly 40 percent of the estimated 14.5 million people who played the game on a regular basis in 1991 were female, according to figures released by the Soccer Industry Council of America. Nearly 5,000 high schools across the country had girls' soccer programs, and 348 NCAA schools had womens' soccer teams, as did 93 NAIA schools and 52 junior colleges.

The roots of this growing involvement go back to the 1920s. In the fall of 1927, a girl named Slacia Penata played regular goalkeeper for the Central Falls, Rhode Island Senior Amateur club. It is highly possible that she was influenced by the United States appearance of Dick Kerr's ladies professional soccer team in 1922. These skilled English players won three games, tied three, and lost two against top men's amateur clubs on the Eastern Seaboard. They outscored the opposition 35-34 and proved that women could excel at the game, too.

Also in the 1920s, Alfredda Inglehart, the first woman admitted to the Soccer Hall of Fame, began her 30-year teaching career in athletics, during which she taught more than 1,200 boys the fundamentals of the game. Many became top-flight professionals, and another, Millard Lang, also became a member of the U.S. Soccer Hall of Fame.

It was not until the early 1960s, however, that girls began playing soccer in any appreciable numbers. Mixed leagues were formed at first, but now more and more girls have leagues of their own. The sport also is increasingly available in high schools and colleges. The governing bodies for college athletics, the NCAA and the NAIA, have conducted postseason tournaments to determine a national soccer champion for women since the early 1980s.

A breakthrough of sorts for women's soccer occurred in October of 1978, when the Sting, a team of 16-20 year olds, placed third in a world tournament in Taipei, Taiwan. The team, based in Dallas, consisted of players from around the country.

The full impact of years of growth was finally felt in August of 1991, when the U.S. team won the women's world championship, outscoring its opponents 25-6 while winning all six games. The team, a mix of U.S. collegians and professionals who were playing in European leagues, defeated Norway in the final game before 60,000 fans in Guangzhou, China. It was the first major international championship for any U.S. soccer team.

The world's championship showed, however, that women's soccer is not yet viewed as equal to men's soccer. Officials considered using a junior-sized ball, an idea that was dropped, and the games were shortened from 90 minutes to 80 because of doubts about the endurance of the women.

Still, without question, the growth of women's soccer in the United States has at the very least kept pace with the men's game.

The Olympics

Soccer's presence in the Olympic Games was slow to develop. Exhibition games were played in the first modern Olympiad, at Athens in 1896, and again at Paris in 1900. The 1904 Games in St. Louis featured informal competition between three teams from the United States and Canada.

After the formation of FIFA, soccer became an official part of the Olympic program beginning with the 1908 Games in London. The United States did not participate in those Games, nor the 1912 Games in Stockholm, because it was not represented by one national governing body, as one of the bylaws in FIFA's constitution demanded.

After the American Football Association and American Amateur Football Association settled their differences and formed the United States Football Association, the U.S. was eligible for Olympic competition. Preparations began immediately to send a team to the 1916 Games in Berlin, Germany. That Olympiad was canceled, however, after World War I broke out.

The U.S. Football Association did not attempt to send a team to the 1920 Games, but another effort was mounted to prepare a team for the 1924 Games in Paris. Soccer experts from across the country sent recommendations of team members and a tryout was held in Paterson, New Jersey. The final roster was an all-star team of the best amateur players in the country. It included no professionals or collegians.

George Mathew Collins of Boston, the soccer editor of the Boston *Daily Globe*, was appointed manager and coach of the Olympic squad. Collins was a great enthusiast of the game. After receiving a broken leg while playing one year, Collins

George Mathew Collins, coach of the 1924 United States Olympic team.

continued to play for another five years under the name of George Mathews so that his wife would not know he still was playing.

The U.S. team had never played together when it sailed for Europe on May 10th on the S.S. America. The squad engaged in two training sessions a day, morning and afternoon, aboard the ship. Calisthenics and gym work occupied the morning sessions while the players worked on heading, trapping, shooting and jogging in the afternoon.

After arriving at Cherbourg, France on May 19th, the team headed for the Olympic village in Paris. The living quarters and food were poor, however, so after one sleepless night arrangements were made to house the team at a hotel 30 minutes from Paris.

The U.S. defeated Estonia in a first-round game on May 25th, 1-0. Andy Straden scored the only goal on a penalty kick while Douglas, the American goalkeeper, shut out the Estonians despite a barrage of goal attempts. Estonia was awarded a penalty kick in the second half, but Kajot put the ball over the crossbar and the Americans heaved a sigh of relief. The referee, however, ordered the kick retaken, claiming he had not blown his whistle. Kajot hit the crossbar on the second chance, but Douglas gathered in the rebound.

The Americans played a physical game to protect their lead, holding, tripping and pushing when necessary. The French fans, already upset over the U.S. victory over the French rugby team the previous day, were very partisan toward the Estonians and showered the U.S. team with boos, hisses and whistling.

The second-round opponent for the U.S. team was Uruguay, a powerful squad that had crushed France in its opening game, 5-1. The Americans would have to play without two regulars who had been injured — Dr. Brix, a clever forward who had suffered a punctured kidney against Estonia, and Rudd, a fullback who had injured an ankle during practice.

The game, played on June 5th, attracted 20,000 fans. The Uruguay team, which included several professional players, scored two goals in the first 15 minutes, then another before halftime to take a 3-0 lead. The U.S. missed several scoring opportunities.

The 1924 U.S. Olympic team, which defeated Estonia before losing to Uruguay. Front row: Burford (trainer), Findley, Brix, Straden, Farrell, Dalrymple. Back row: Davis, Rudd, Peel (USSF President), Douglas, Jones, Hornberger, O'Connor, Collins (coach).

In the second half, Coach Collins made a strategic move that preceded by a quarter of a century the Swiss "Verrou" and the Italian "Catenaccio" systems, which emphasized defense. In an effort to hold the clever Uruguay attack in check, Collins played the sweeper behind a line of four backs. This move helped prevent the South Americans from scoring in the second half, but the U.S. team could not score either, and lost 3-0. Ironically, the French crowd cheered the American team after this game for its valiant effort. Uruguay went on to win the gold medal, outscoring its opponents 20-2.

The United States team played two post-tournament games before departing for home. On June 10th, it defeated Poland 3-2 at Warsaw before an enthusiastic and friendly crowd. It then lost to the Irish Free State team in Dublin on June 14, 3-1.

As Coach Collins reported to the United States Football Association, the American team made a remarkable showing considering the conditions. Most of the clubs in the Olympic competition had been playing together for a year or two with subsidized "amateur" players. Uruguay had maintained the same squad for four years and played 11 games in Europe prior to the opening of the tournament.

Most of the Olympic Games that followed were not so encouraging for the U.S. teams, however.

At the 1928 Games in Amsterdam, Holland, the Americans lost to Italy in the first round, 11-2. Uruguay won the gold medal, just as it had in 1924.

The 1932 Games in Los Angeles provided a tremendous opportunity for soccer followers in the United States. Amateur soccer had reached a high standard by this time, and a solid performance by an American team would have boosted the sport's image in the United States considerably. The sport was not included on the Olympic schedule that year, however, because many countries could not afford to send a team as a result of the Depression and because of disagreements between FIFA and the U.S. Olympic Committee. It was a major setback for the game in the U.S.

This circumstance and the emergence of World Cup play in 1930 combined to lessen the importance of soccer in Olympic competition, particularly in the United States.

The United States displayed unsuspected strength in the Olympic Games of 1936 at Berlin, Germany. Heavy snowfalls during the previous winter had all but ruined the exhibition games that were to raise funds and provide the players an opportunity to play together before leaving the United States.

The U.S. team drew the Italians, who were favored to win the gold medal, for its first-round opponent. Many of the Italian players were professionals (although they officially were declared students) and they played a physical, aggressive game that the American players considered beneath the rules. Two U.S. players were injured during the game — one was hit in the mouth, and the other in the groin — but continued to play.

The Italians scored a second-half goal to win 1-0, and went on to capture the gold medal. Still, it was an encouraging performance for the U.S. team. The fact that 14 of the 17 team members were native-born Americans typified the game's growing popularity. Such signs of hope were quickly dashed, however. World War II forced cancellation of the Olympic Games in 1940 and 1944, and the American teams were not competitive in the Olympics that followed.

In 1948, bad weather hampered the fund-raising tour, just as it had in 1936. The Olympic Soccer Committee was left with the task of raising $14,000 for transportation, housing, uniforms and other expenses. Ultimately, each state soccer association had to appeal for money to finance the team.

Again, the players were chosen by a selection committee after a series of international games. And again, the team wound up leaving for the Olympics without the benefit of playing a single game together. The players were put through conditioning exercises on the boat to London and then played exhibition games there before the start of the Games.

Again, however, the U.S. team had poor luck in the draw. It was originally supposed to play Poland, but the Polish team withdrew and the U.S. wound up having to play Italy again. This time the Americans were no match for their favored opponent, losing 9-0.

The defeat emphasized the need for reform in selecting and preparing U.S. teams for the Olympics. While other countries fielded experienced professionals, the U.S. was sending amateurs — and not even the best amateurs. Many of the top college players were not competing in the Olympics because they could not leave school long enough to try out and train.

The 1952 team was selected after a similar process of tryouts, but did have an opportunity to play together before opening Olympic competition. The results were no better, however. Having to play the Italians once again — this time in a qualifying game because of the large number of teams entered — the Americans were embarrassed, 9-0. Italy lost in the second round to Hungary, which went on to win the gold medal.

Walter Giesler, manager of the 1952 Olympic team, cut to the heart of the problems of the U.S. team with a recommendation after the Games. Noting that the better teams from Europe and South America were playing together for as long as six months before the Olympics began and that it was impossible for the American amateurs to do so, Giesler suggested that the Olympic Soccer Committee arrange a match between the national amateur champion and the best collegiate team, with the winner representing the United States in the Olympics.

This advice was not acted upon, however. In preparations for the 1956 Games in Australia, amateur players were given the opportunity to try out in statewide competitions, and then a series of regional games was played to narrow the field to East and West teams that played in the finals of the trials competition in St. Louis. Sixteen team members were chosen from this group.

The Olympic team originally was scheduled to participate in a two-week training period in Los Angeles, but instead played a three-week series of games in the Far East at the invitation of the State Department. This provided ample opportunity to play together, although some thought all the travel and sightseeing left the players too tired to be at their best in the Olympics. In any regard, the Americans lost their first-round game to Yugoslavia, 9-1. Yugoslavia went on to lose to Russia in the gold medal game.

The team that finished third in the 1959 Pan American Games was left intact for the 1960 Olympics under the same coach, James Reed. A preliminary qualifying round was introduced for the Olympics that year, from which 16 teams would compete for the gold medal. This seemed to improve the odds for the American team, because it reduced the chance of losing first-round matches to outstanding opponents.

The U.S. team did not prepare well for the trials, however. It arrived in Mexico two days before the qualifying game against the Mexican team without having trained or played together since the Pan American Games. It did not have a field for practice upon reaching Mexico, and could not even run in a public park because water was running out of a septic tank. The Americans went on to lose, 2-0.

PHOTO BY KENT PHILLIPS

A member of the 1992 United States Olympic team heads the ball during a trials match against a team from Canada.

More than a month later, the two teams met again in Los Angeles. Still ill-prepared, the U.S. team tied the Mexicans, 1-1. Mexico went on to compete in the Olympics, while the Americans stayed home.

The U.S. team failed to qualify for the 1964 Olympics as well. Competing in the preliminary round with three other North American teams — Mexico, Surinam and Panama — the U.S. lost to Surinam 1-0 and then defeated Panama 4-2. Facing the Mexican team in the preliminary finals for the right to compete in the Olympics, it lost 2-1.

The U.S. team did not have to worry about beating Mexico to compete in the 1968 Olympics, because Mexico was the host country and an automatic participant. This time, it only had to face Bermuda in the preliminary round of the North American zone.

Again, however, the team was poorly managed. The 18 team members who had been chosen from tryouts in various regions of the country scrimmaged a few times against local competition, but the team did not have a structured training period. Also, the team's coach, Geza Henni, did not get along well with the U.S. manager, Walter Giesler, who wanted a voice in determining who played.

The first game in Bermuda ended in a 1-1 tie. The Americans lost the second game, played at Comiskey Park in Chicago, 1-0, and again failed to advance to the Olympics.

A breakthrough of sorts came in 1972. Guelker, the veteran coach at St. Louis University, took over the team, which consisted entirely of collegiate players, and put it through an organized, disciplined training session. This time, however, the team would have to survive two qualifying rounds.

It defeated Barbados twice and tied El Salvador twice, setting up a playoff match with El Salvador for the right to advance to the second round. That game went to overtime, and then had to be decided by penalty kicks. The U.S. was leading 5-4 on kicks when Shep Messing, the American goalie, called upon a bit of psychological warfare. Messing, a Harvard student, began stomping around the goal net, tearing at his shirt and screaming insults at the El Salvador player who was waiting to take his shot. The ploy worked, as the Salvadoran sent the kick above the crossbar. The U.S. won and advanced to the second round along with Mexico, Jamaica and Guatemala.

The Americans won one game, lost one and tied three in the second round. They then played the deciding game against Jamaica in St. Louis and won 2-1, to advance to the Olympic Games. They also got a small measure of revenge against Mexico in the process, tying the Mexicans and eliminating them from the qualifying round.

At the Olympics in Munich, the U.S. team played Morocco to a scoreless tie and then lost to Malaysia 3-0. That left it in a near-hopeless situation. To advance to the next round, it would have had to defeat a powerful West German team by seven goals. Guelker decided to admit defeat and play his reserves so that they could experience the thrill of Olympic competition. The U.S. lost 7-0, and needed an incredible 62 saves from Messing to accomplish that.

The United States team failed to qualify for the 1976 Olympics in Montreal. It split two games with Bermuda in the preliminary round, but advanced because it scored more goals. It had to play Mexico in the second round, and the Mexicans avenged the tie that had eliminated them in 1972 with an 8-0 victory in Mexico. The return match was played four days later in Wilmington, Delaware, and the U.S. lost 4-2 to end its qualifying bid.

The United States and many of its allies boycotted the 1980 Olympics in Moscow. The U.S. team had qualifed for the Games by advancing past Surinam, Costa Rica, Bermuda and Mexico (by forfeit). Czechoslovakia won the gold medal over East Germany, 1-0, while the Soviet Union placed third.

As the host country, the United States team was an automatic qualifier for the 1984 Olympics in Los Angeles, which were marred by, the boycott of the games by the Soviet Union and other Communist nations. The U.S. defeated Costa Rica 3-0, tied Egypt and then lost to Italy. France won the gold medal, defeating Brazil in the championship game, 2-0.

The U.S. qualified again for the 1988 Olympics in Seoul, Korea. It split games with Canada and defeated Trinidad and El Salvador in the qualifying rounds. In the Olympics, it played a scoreless tie with South Korea and lost to the Soviet Union, 4-2. Russia went on to win the gold medal, defeating Brazil in the final game.

5

The World Cup

The World Cup is, quite simply, the biggest sporting event in the world. It attracts more spectators — as many as 200,000 in person and billions more on worldwide television — than any other event.

Held every four years, the tournament is open to all FIFA members and is the showcase for the sport. It is considered the most important soccer competition in the world, even greater than the Olympics. It also is riddled with political interference, controversy and violence, a reflection of the passions that run so deep throughout the game.

Talk of a world's soccer championship began in 1904 when FIFA was organized. The tournament didn't become a reality, however, until 1930. During the 1920s, the issue of amateurism in international competition became more controversial as some countries interpreted it more loosely than others. While some provided their players only travel expenses and housing, others paid bonus money and other compensation.

In response to the growing disenchantment, FIFA officials at their meeting in 1926 in Rome proposed an open world's championship that would not have the qualifying restrictions of the Olympics. Two years later, at a meeting during the Olympics in Amsterdam, the idea was approved by a large majority of the members, although the British Isles withdrew from FIFA because of their support for the traditional spirit of amateurism.

Five countries — Italy, Holland, Spain, Sweden and Uruguay — were considered as candidates to host the first tournament. Uruguay, which had won the two previous Olympic gold medals and was to celebrate its 100th year of independence in 1930, was chosen. The other four countries immediately refused to participate, providing

The U.S. team that played in the first World Cup in Montevideo Uruguay in 1930. Front row: James Brown, Philip Sloan. Second row: Raphael "Ralph" Tracey, James Gallagher, Mike Bookie, Thomas Florie (captain), Bert Patenaude, Arnie Oliver, Bart McGhee. Third row: Elmer Schoeder (assistant manager), Wilfred Cummings (manager), Alexander Wood, James Gentle, George Moorhouse, James Douglas, Billy Gonsalves, Frank Vaughn, Andrew Auld, Robert Millar (coach), Jack Coll (trainer).

the first hint of the political intrigue that would shadow the tournament throughout its history. Austria, Czechoslovakia, Germany, Hungary and Switzerland also were unable to send teams.

In all, 13 countries participated. Uruguay built a new stadium and offered to pay the travel and lodging expenses for the teams from Europe, a huge sacrifice for a poor nation. This World Cup was the only one that had no qualifying rounds. All the teams that entered qualified automatically and played in Montevideo.

Uruguay won the championship, defeating Argentina in the final game, 4-2, in a rematch of the 1928 Olympics between the two South American countries. More than 100,000 spectators filled the new stadium to watch the game, chanting "Victory or death!"

Sportsmanship did not reign supreme. Emotions were running so high that the referee who worked the championship game agreed to do so only after his life was insured. The two teams also argued over what kind of ball to use. It was decided to use the Argentine ball the first half and the Uruguay ball in the second half. Perhaps not coincidentally, Argentina took a 2-1 lead at the half, but Uruguay came back in the second half to win.

PHOTO COURTESY NATIONAL SOCCER HALL OF FAME

Harry Keough attempts to score against England's Frank Borghi during the 1950 World Cup. Keough went on to become a successful coach at St. Louis University.

A national holiday was declared in Uruguay after the victory. Angry Argentines, meanwhile, threw rocks at the Uruguayan consulate until policemen fired guns to scatter them.

The U.S. team, which featured several former British professionals from the American Soccer League, performed surprisingly well. It defeated Belgium and Paraguay, but lost to Argentina, 6-1, in the semifinals after trailing just 1-0 at the half. It, too, was involved in controversy, however. The Americans argued that Argentina's players were far more physical than the rules permitted. Ralph Tracy suffered a broken leg in the first half. Substitutions were not allowed at the time (a rule that would hold until 1970), so the U.S. team had to continue with 10 players. Goalie Jimmy Douglas was kicked in the head and left half Andy Auld was hit in the mouth. Both played, but were ineffective because of the injuries.

• • •

The 1934 World Cup, played in Italy, was even more political. Benito Mussolini, the Italian dictator, declared his country would win beforehand, and passed a ruling that helped accomplish his prediction. Any player born abroad of Italian parents could play for Italy, he said. This enabled him to add a few Argentine players to his team,

The 1950 United States World Cup team, which pulled a legendary upset of England in Belo Horizonte, Brazil. Front row: Frank Wallace, Ed McIlveney, Gino Pariani, Joe Gaetjens, John Souza, Edward Souza. Back row: Wilian Lyons, assistant coach, Joe Maca, Charley Colombo, Frank Borghi, Harry Keough, Walter Bahr, Bill Jeffrey, coach.

including one who had played for Argentina in the 1930 World Cup. This issue became increasingly controversial in World Cup play. Thirty years later, FIFA finally passed a rule stating that participants must be citizens of the country they represent and cannot have played for another country's team in previous tournaments.

The Italian team was sent to the country six weeks prior to the tournament to train under the strict guidance of Vittorio Pozzo, one of the game's great coaches. He helped get his players in a competitive frame of mind by promising them large cash bonuses if they won the championship.

The United States won a preliminary game over Mexico, 4-2, as Tom Florie scored three goals. The Americans had to play Italy in the opening round, however, with Mussolini and 30,000 other spectators looking on. Italy, unleashed from its rigorous training camp, dismissed the United States 7-1. It could have been worse if not for the stellar play of the American goalie, Julius Julian.

Italy went on to eliminate Spain 1-0 in a replay of a tie game, and then defeated Czechoslovakia in overtime in the final, 2-1. Mussolini and the home fans were jubilant over the victory, but many observers believed the Czechs had been the superior team.

• • •

The 1938 World Cup in France had a much different look, and reflected the tense world situation of the time. Austria, which had advanced to the semifinals in 1934, had temporarily ceased to exist, having been absorbed by Hitler's expanding empire. Spain was immersed in a civil war. The United States failed to qualify. Argentina, angry over not getting to host the tournament and the fact Italy had taken some of its better players, refused to participate. So did Uruguay, which still was bitter over the fact the European countries had not participated when it hosted the tournament in 1930. And England, still embroiled in a dispute with FIFA, continue to boycott the event.

Italy and Germany were co-favorites to win the tournament. Italy had added a member of Uruguay's team, another foreign-born "Italian," and Germany had added former members of the Austrian team. Brazil also had an outstanding team that featured Leonidas, the "Black Diamond." He is credited with being the first player to use the overhead scissors kick.

PHOTO COURTESY NATIONAL SOCCER HALL OF FAME

Roy Bentley of England and Harry Keough of the United States try to head the ball during 1950 World Cup action. Other players, from left, are John Souza, Charley Colombo, Walt Bahr and Ed McIlveney, all of the United States.

The Germans were upset by Switzerland in the first round, while the Italians narrowly escaped with a 2-1 overtime victory over Norway. The highlight was Brazil's first-round victory over Poland, which is considered one of the great World Cup matches of all time. Leonidas scored four goals to lead his team to a 6-5 overtime victory, while Poland's Ernest Willimowski also scored four goals.

Brazil then played Czechoslovakia to a 1-1 tie that featured several ejections and serious injuries. Brazil came back to win the replay, 2-1, but had to face Italy in the semifinals without Leonidas. Some reports stated that he had a knee injury, while others said he was held out by his coach to rest for the finals. In any regard, Italy defeated Brazil, 2-1, and then beat Hungary for the championship, 4-2.

• • •

World War II forced cancellation of the World Cup until 1950, when the tournament resumed in Brazil. This Cup marked the first entrance of England, which had joined FIFA in 1946. The English had dominated international soccer play in the late 1940s and were considered one of the favorites to win the championship.

They did not, thanks to one of the biggest upsets in the tournament's history and probably the greatest moment in the history of U.S. soccer. The United States team, made up mostly of native-born, semi-professional players, prepared rather seriously for the tournament. It also had ample motivation. The mere reputation of the English professionals was enough to get their attention. A warning issued by the president of the British soccer federation also lit a spark. After the U.S. team performed well in an exhibition match against a touring English team shortly before leaving for Brazil, Stanley Rous, speaking at a banquet in New York City, noted the English players were fatigued from their travels and declared: "When you go to Brazil and play the English national team, then you will find out what football is all about."

The U.S. team played surprisingly well in its first match, but lost 3-1 to Spain. (That year, the World Cup was not single-elimination. Four divisions were established, with the winning team from each division playing in the finals.) The U.S. then played England, a team nobody following the World Cup figured could lose to the Americans. The only question seemed to be how many goals the English would score, not if they would win.

The English, who had defeated Chile without much trouble in their first match, arrived in Belo Horizonte a few days before the game and rested and practiced in a settlement of Englishmen who worked in a nearby gold mine. The Americans arrived the day before the game and did not get to practice at all. The English, disdainful of the cramped dressing quarters, changed in their hotel rooms and took a bus to the stadium. The U.S. team dressed at the stadium, hanging their clothes on nails.

England held out one of its standout players, Stanley Matthews, to rest him for later games — an indication of its confidence. Perhaps it was overconfident. The U.S. team won, 1-0, on a legendary goal off the head of center forward Joe Gaetjens in the first half.

Descriptions of Gaetjens' goal vary. Some British reporters wrote that it was an accident, that he merely got in the way of a shot by teammate Walter Bahr. The best evidence, however, is that Gaetjens, a reckless player by nature, dove for the ball and redirected it past the surprised goalie. Bahr was indeed shooting the ball, not passing it, but most observers believe Gaetjens made a great play.

England still had plenty of time to tie the game. It got off several shots on goal, but most of them were inaccurate. The U.S. goalie, Frank Borghi, played the game of his life in stopping the rest. The Americans also were said to get away with a few fouls in the second half that prevented English scoring opportunities. In any regard, the U.S. team held on for the shocking upset. One newspaper reporter called it "the biggest shock in the history of international football."

The Brazilian fans, who had cheered for the Americans because England was considered one of Brazil's primary challengers for the championship, went wild. They lit firecrackers, set fire to newspapers and jumped the moat surrounding the field to hug and carry off the stunned Americans.

The Associated Press dispatch of June 29th, 1950 was clear and concise. It read:

> "The United States today defeated England 1-0 to add the latest and biggest upset in the world soccer championships. The favored British team and the spectators were stunned by the result. The lone tally of the match was scored by Joe Gaetjens at 39 minutes of the first half.

> "Brazilian fans swarmed onto the field after the United States victory and took the Americans on their shoulders while the victors were given an ovation."

The U.S. team could not come back down to earth in time after the victory, however. It lost its next game, 5-2 to Chile in its next game. Still, it returned home with one of the most memorable victories in World Cup history. It would be 40 years before another United States team qualified for the World Cup.

Eight of the players on the American team were native born. McIlvenny, a Scotsman, Maca, a Belgian and Gaetjens, a Haitian, were the only members who were foreign born. Technically they were not American citizens, however, and all three returned to their native countries shortly after the tournament.

(The legend surrounding Gaetjens has grown over the years because of his mysterious disappearance. He played in France following the 1950 World Cup, then returned to Haiti in 1953. He was last seen on July 8, 1964 with a gun held to his head by a member of the secret police. He had been charged with subversive activity, as had his brothers.

Clive Toye, then general manager of the New York Cosmos, launched a world-wide effort to locate Gaetjens in the early 1970s, but had no success. To the best of anyone's knowledge, Gaetjens was killed by the police in Haiti.)

The celebration the Brazilian fans began after the U.S. team's victory over England ended a bit prematurely. Their nation's team advanced to the final game against Uruguay, and more than 200,000 fans filled the new Maracanã Stadium in Rio de Janeiro awaiting the expected championship. Victory seemed almost assured when Brazil took a 1-0 lead early in the second half, but Uruguay exhibited superior teamwork and aggressiveness toward the end of the game and won, 2-1.

● ● ●

The 1954 World Cup, played in Switzerland, also featured an upset in the final game. Hungary had not been defeated in four seasons, including the 1952 Olympics, and was the heavy favorite. After it beat Korea 9-0 in its first game, it appeared invincible.

West Germany, however, had a plan. After defeating Turkey, the West Germans played seven reserves when they met Hungary. They lost, 8-3, but fooled the Hungarians into thinking they had a weak team. That was important because the two teams would meet again. (The tournament format, while different than in 1950, still was a complicated system that made it possible for a team to lose an early-round game but remain eligible for the championship.)

The semifinal rounds of this World Cup featured games that showed both the best and worst the event has to offer. Hungary's 4-2 victory over Brazil became known as "The Battle of Berne" as both teams engaged in illegal tactics in one of the ugliest, most violent displays in the history of international soccer. Three players, two from Brazil and one from Hungary, were kicked out of the game for rough play. Fights broke out on the field and again in the locker room afterward. The angry Brazilians threatened to kill the referee, an Englishman, if he ever stepped foot in their country.

Hungary's next game, against Uruguay, turned out to be one of the highlights of World Cup play. Both teams played a clean, aggressive game that many still consider the best match ever played in the tournament. Uruguay overcame a 2-0 deficit to force an overtime, but Hungary held on for a 4-2 victory.

Hungary then played the West Germans, whom they had defeated so easily a week earlier, in the final game. This time, however, the West Germans went with their best players. Playing aggressively and consistently on a rain-soaked field, the West Germans overcame a 2-0 deficit and won, 3-2. It was the only loss the Hungarians would suffer over a 49-game stretch from 1950-56.

Another notable event in the tournament was the June 16 match between France and Yugoslavia. It was the first World Cup game ever televised.

• • •

The 1958 World Cup in Sweden featured the debut of a 17-year-old Brazilian named Edson Arantes do Nascimento. In later years he would become known as Pelé, and without question rank as the most famous athlete in the world — perhaps the most famous *person* in the world.

Brazil, ranked as one of the heavy favorites entering the tournament, was unimpressive in a 3-0 first-round victory over Austria, and was even less impressive in its next game, a scoreless tie with England. After that game, the Brazilian players talked their coach, Vicente Feola, into starting the new kid, Pelé, who had not played at all the first two games.

A legend was born. Pelé played well in Brazil's impressive 2-0 victory over Russia, which was making its first World Cup appearance, and then scored the game's only goal in a 1-0 victory over Wales, another first- time competitor.

He went on to score three goals in a 5-2 victory over France in the semifinals and added two more in a 5-2 win over host Sweden in the championship game.

Pelé collapsed on the field in tears after the game ended. His teammates carried him on their shoulders as they ran a victory lap around the field. They held aloft a Swedish flag as well, to the approval of the fans. Sweden's king even happily posed for a picture with the Brazilian players. It was a rare moment of goodwill in World Cup play.

• • •

Brazil repeated its championship in the 1962 World Cup in Chile. This tournament wasn't as peaceful as the previous one, however.

An Italian journalist got the proceedings off to a bad start when he wrote a negative article about the host country before play began. When Italy played Chile, play was extremely rough. It was reported that a Chilean player took a swing at an Italian, and the referee responded by kicking two Italian players out of the game.

Pelé pulled a muscle during the second game and had to miss the rest of the tournament, but Brazil continued onward. Its most difficult game was in the semifinals against Chile. One of Brazil's star players, Garrincha, was fouled repeatedly. When he retaliated, he was ejected from the game. He was not expected to be able to play in the championship match, but the President of Brazil appealed to FIFA officials and requested leniency. Whether bowing to this request or the wishes of the fans, FIFA allowed Garrincha to play.

Garrincha did not play well in the final against Czechoslovakia, but Brazil broke a 1-1 halftime tie and went on to win anyway, 3-1. The surprising play of the Czechoslovakians, however, was one of the bright spots of the tournament.

• • •

The 1966 World Cup in England also had its share of ugly happenings. Italy, one of the favorites to win the championship, was upset by North Korea, a newcomer to international competition, 1-0 in first-round play. It was a shock much like the U.S. team's defeat of England in 1950. The Italian fans were so angry over the loss that the team took an alternate route on its way home, flying into the airport in Genoa rather than Rome. Still, a mob of fans greeted the players by throwing tomatoes at them.

Brazil, meanwhile, was upset by Portugal, which featured Eusebio, a player billed as "the new Pelé." Eusebio scored two goals in Portugal's 3-1 victory. Pelé, meanwhile, was the victim of rough play, and vowed afterward he would never again play in the World Cup. By the time the next one rolled around, however, he had changed his mind.

England won the tournament, becoming the third host team to do so. It played a defensive-oriented style that kept the scores low and produced little excitement, but the home fans didn't mind.

It's final-game victory over West Germany, which featured 21-year-old Franz Beckenbauer, was different. Playing before 100,000 fans at Wembley Stadium and 400 million on worldwide television, the two teams played a fast-paced, aggressive game. Geoff Hurst scored three goals — becoming the first player in World Cup history to do so — two of them in overtime to lead England to a 4-2 victory.

This World Cup also was noted for a famous act of theft. The World Cup itself — the Jules Rimet Trophy, named after a Frenchman who had been a founder and past president of FIFA — was stolen before the tournament began from London's Central Hall, despite the fact six security guards had been assigned to protect it.

The solid gold cup had cost $6,000 when it was made in 1930, but was worth far more than that to the teams who won it. The legend surrounding it had grown immensely during World War II when a member of the Italian Football Federation buried it to protect it from the occupying German soldiers.

As it turned out, the trophy was buried again. One day as a man named Corbett and his dog Pickles were walking through a London suburb, Pickles happened to dig up the trophy.

• • •

Brazil retired the trophy after the 1970 World Cup in Mexico by winning for the third time. This was the last World Cup tournament for Pelé, who at 30 years old still ranked as one of the best players in the world.

This tournament featured some of the best soccer in World Cup history, despite the high altitude. Brazil breezed through the competition on its way to the finals, having difficulty only in a 1-0 victory over England. It met Italy in the championship match and won easily, 4-1. Pelé was outstanding throughout the competition, and the Brazilian offense was merciless; it scored 19 goals in six games.

Brazil's hold on the trophy wasn't as eternal as it was supposed to be, however. It was stolen in 1983 and never recovered. Brazilian police suspect that it was melted down.

• • •

The tournament format was changed for the 1974 World Cup. Quarterfinal and semifinal rounds were eliminated and the top two teams from each of the four groups were divided into two more groups. The winner of each of those played for the championship.

West Germany, the host team, won the title in another well-played tournament, but Holland and Poland also performed well. Holland, led by Johann Cruyff and Johan Neeskens, outscored its opponents 14-1 on its way to the finals. Poland, which had won the 1972 Olympics, breezed past Argentina, Haiti, Italy, Sweden and Yugoslavia before losing to West Germany on a rain-soaked field in the final game. Many thought the game should not have been played because of the poor playing conditions.

Holland took a 1-0 lead on Neeskens' penalty kick, the result of a foul committed against Cruyff, but the Dutch team backed off its attack after its goal. Gerd Muller scored the winning goal for the West Germans, becoming the all-time World Cup scoring leader with 14 goals.

• • •

The host team won again in 1978 as Argentina, the birthplace of soccer in South America, won its first championship. The tournament was tense from the beginning, as a succession of Argentinian leaders were overthrown, and the president of the Argentine World Cup Organizing Committee was assassinated two years before play began. Ultimately, the tournament proceeded successfully and without incident.

Some of the stars of past World Cups, most notably Cruyff and Beckenbauer, did not compete. Beckenbauer was playing professionally in the United States. Cruyff cited personal reasons for his absence, but Holland advanced to the final game anyway before losing 3-1.

One of the standouts of the tournament was Italy's Paolo Rossi, who led his team to victories over Argentina, France and Hungary before it was eliminated.

• • •

The Italians came back to win the 1982 World Cup in Spain. The tournament's format was changed again, as the field was increased to 24 qualifying teams and the competition spanned nearly a month.

Rossi again was the standout player, although a belated one. He was held scoreless through Italy's first four games and was benched twice for his uninspired play. He came back to score three goals to lead the Italians into the semifinals, then added two more against Poland as they advanced to the championship game against West Germany.

Rossi scored the first goal of the final game — his sixth goal of the tournament — and Italy went on to a 3-1 victory. It was the third World Cup championship for the Italians, tying them with Brazil for most titles.

• • •

Rossi was replaced in the limelight by a new star, Argentina's Diego Maradona, in the 1986 World Cup in Mexico.

Maradona had played in the 1982 World Cup as a 21-year-old, and gained notoriety by getting ejected from a game for committing a violent foul. He would become better known in 1986 for scoring a controversial goal and for leading his team to the championship.

During Argentina's quarterfinal match with England, Maradona and the English goalie, Peter Shilton, jumped for a ball near the goal. Maradona somehow deflected the ball into the net for a goal, but replays showed he illegally punched it with his left fist rather than his head. Asked about it afterward, he gave credit to "the hand of God."

Maradona scored both goals in the 2-1 win over England, and two more in a 2-0 victory over Belgium in the semifinals. He also contributed a beautiful assist to Jorge Burruchaga with just six minutes left for the winning goal in Argentina's 3-2 win over West Germany in the championship game.

• • •

The 1990 World Cup in Italy marked the return of the United States to tournament play for the first time since 1950. The Americans endured a long, difficult qualifying process, defeating Trinidad and Tobago on its home field to reach the field of competitors.

The U.S. team did not fare well in the tournament, however. It played poorly in its first game, losing to Czechoslovakia in the first round, 5- 1. It returned four nights later to turn in an impressive performance against host Italy, but lost 1-0 before 73,000 fans. It lost its third game as well, 2-1 to Austria.

West Germany won the championship, defeating Argentina in a memorable final game, 1-0. Beckenbauer, now the West German coach, assembled a strong team that was able to take the last step that had barely eluded the teams in 1982 and 1986. The West Germans dominated the game, getting off 16 shots on goal to Argentina's one. Andreas Brehme scored the game's only goal on a penalty kick.

The Argentine players reacted vehemently to the defeat. Already angry over the officiating — two of their team members had been ejected from the game in the second half — they rushed the field afterward and verbally assaulted the referee. It took several minutes before order was restored and the awards ceremony could begin. Maradona, crying, left the field without shaking hands with FIFA President Joao Havelange and before the West Germans received their medals and trophy.

West Germany's championship was its third in World Cup play, tying it with Brazil and Italy for the most tournaments won. The West Germans have reached six finals, eight semifinals and played in 10 tournaments since World War II. Their overall World Cup record of 38 wins, 14 losses and 10 ties ranks second only to Brazil's mark of 48-12-13.

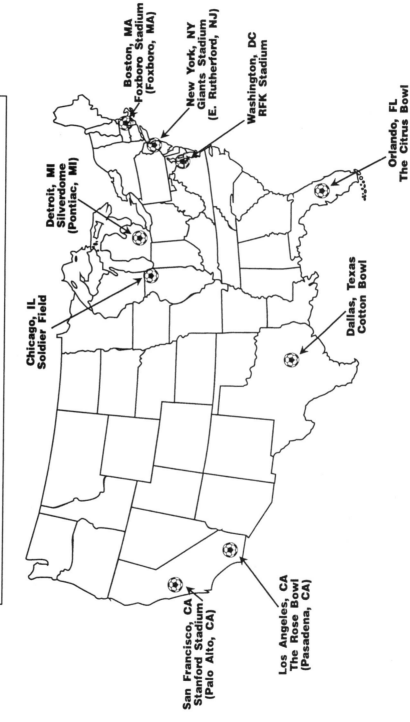

1994 FIFA WORLD CUP VENUES

Boston, MA
Foxboro Stadium
(Foxboro, MA)

New York, NY
Giants Stadium
(E. Rutherford, NJ)

Washington, DC
RFK Stadium

Orlando, FL
The Citrus Bowl

Detroit, MI
Silverdome
(Pontiac, MI)

Chicago, IL
Soldier Field

Dallas, Texas
Cotton Bowl

San Francisco, CA
Stanford Stadium
(Palo Alto, CA)

Los Angeles, CA
The Rose Bowl
(Pasadena, CA)

6

World Cup 1994

The scoreboard in Rome's Olympic Stadium flashed this sign at the conclusion of the 1990 World Cup: Ciao, Italia '90 Hello, USA 1994

The United States was awarded the 1994 tournament on July 4, 1988. Many consider this the greatest moment in the sport's history in the U.S., and an opportunity for the sport to win new fans — an even greater opportunity than the one that was lost when the sport was not included in the 1932 Olympic Games in Los Angeles.

The World Cup will be played from June 17 through July 17 in or just outside of nine major cities throughout the United States: Boston, Chicago, Dallas, Detroit, Los Angeles, New York, Orlando, San Francisco and Washington, D.C. These cities were chosen from the 27 who submitted formal bids. The championship match will be played near Detroit at the Pontiac Silverdome, and will be the first World Cup match ever played indoors.

FIFA's demand that all World Cup matches be played on grass has forced an interesting innovation, one that might eventually impact football and baseball games played indoors. Grass will be grown inside the Silverdome, the first time this has been tried for a major sporting event in an indoor stadium since the Houston Astrodome opened in 1965.

The process, which will cost more than $1 million to implement, was developed by Michigan State University specialists. The grass — a hybrid mixture — will be grown in containers about 10 feet long, five feet wide and six inches deep. These modules will then be mounted on wheels and carted into the Silverdome. Mobile banks of halogen lamps will be placed six to eight feet above the surface to amplify the sunlight already coming through the stadium's roof. If the grass still fails to grow, the modules can be moved outdoors between games.

The final pool of 24 teams will be taken from the largest field of entrants in World Cup history. A total of 143 teams entered the qualifying competition, breaking the record of 123 set in 1990. They will play nearly 600 matches from January 1992 to November 1993 to determine which 22 teams advance to the final competition. (The United States, as the host country, and West Germany, as the defending champion, qualify automatically.)

After the field of 24 is set, a draw will be held in December of 1993 to determine the matchups and sites of the first-round games. Six of the strongest teams are seeded and placed at the head of each of six groups; the remaining three spots in each group are filled by a draw, although measures are taken to ensure that not too many teams from the same region of the world are placed in the same group.

After the six groups of four teams are established, each team plays the other three teams in its group. Each group winner and runner-up advance to the second round along with the four top third-place teams. The group standings are determined on a point system which awards two points for a victory, one for a tie and none for a loss.

From the second round on, the tournament is single-elimination. The two semi-final losers meet the day before the championship game to determine the third-place finisher.

The Americans were the youngest team to compete in the 1990 World Cup, and many of the same players will return for the 1994 competition. The U.S. team's status as an automatic qualifier is both a blessing and a curse, however. Although it does not have to risk elimination in the qualifying rounds, the experience gained during the qualifying rounds can be a valuable asset in the actual tournament.

Part II: Rules

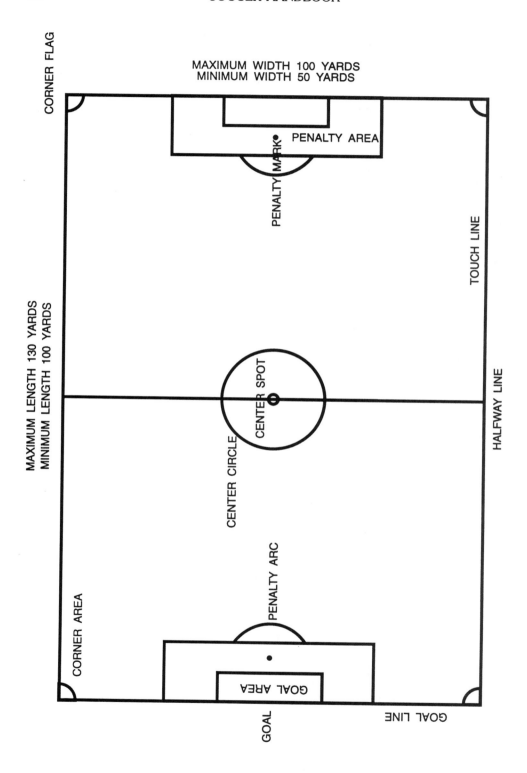

MAXIMUM WIDTH 100 YARDS
MINIMUM WIDTH 50 YARDS

CORNER FLAG

PENALTY AREA

PENALTY MARK

TOUCH LINE

MAXIMUM LENGTH 130 YARDS
MINIMUM LENGTH 100 YARDS

CENTER SPOT

CENTER CIRCLE

HALFWAY LINE

PENALTY ARC

CORNER AREA

GOAL AREA

GOAL

GOAL LINE

7

The Laws of Soccer

Until 1992, the 17 laws of soccer had changed little since 1863. Minor adjustments were made from time to time under FIFA's jurisdiction, but only rarely and only uniformly. However, on May 30, 1992, the International Football Association made changes that greatly affect the game. These changes, which primarily govern laws 5, 12, 13 and 16, were to go into effect in late 1992 or early 1993.

High schools, colleges and professional leagues in the United States alter the rules to fit their needs, but all adult international games are played by the same set of rules.

The rules that follow are presented in simplified form. The official text of the rules is available from FIFA by way of the United States Soccer Federation at 1750 E. Boulder St., Colorado Springs, CO, 80909.

LAW I: FIELD

The length of the field may range from 100 to 130 yards, and the width from 50 to 100 yards. The touch lines (side boundaries) and goal lines (end boundaries) are part of the playing field, and can be no more than five inches wide.

A flag must be placed on a post five feet high at each corner of the field. Corner areas are designated by quarter circles, three feet from the corner flags.

The goal area extends six yards in front of each goal, and is 20 yards wide. The goals are to be 24 feet wide and eight feet in height. The posts and crossbar may be square, rectangular or round, but must be painted white. Goal nets may be attached to the posts to catch the ball.

The penalty kick mark is 12 yards from the midpoint of the goal line. The penalty area, which includes the goal area, is 44 yards wide and 18 yards deep. The penalty kick arc is outside of the penalty area, and 10 yards from the kick mark.

The center circle is in the center of the field, and has a radius of 10 yards.

LAW II: BALL

The ball must be made of leather or have a leather-like cover and be 27-28 inches in circumference, weigh 14-16 ounces and have 14 pounds of air pressure. (Youth leagues may use smaller balls.)

LAW III: NUMBER OF PLAYERS

Each team shall have no more than 11 players, including the goalkeeper. (Most leagues require at least seven players per team for a game to be official.)

Only two substitutions are allowed per game from a submitted list of five players. (Some leagues allow more substitutions.) A player who has been substituted for cannot re—enter the game. (U.S. youth leagues, high schools and colleges allow re-entry.)

Substitutions may only be made while play is stopped. A substitute must wait for the referee's signal before entering the field of play, and must enter at the halfway line after the player being replaced leaves the field. Injured players may not be replaced if the substitution limit has been reached. If an injured player is not replaced, that player can re-enter the field of play upon the referee's signal, even if the ball is in play. A player who has been ejected by the referee cannot be replaced. That player's team must play with one less player.

Field players can exchange positions with the goalkeeper only when the game is stopped and the referee has been notified. If the referee is not notified, both players are cautioned after the ball is out of play.

Players may not enter or leave the field without the referee's permission except as game situations dictate, such as throw-ins and corner kicks. If a substitute enters the field without permission, the referee should stop play and caution the player. The game is then restarted with a drop ball.

LAW IV: EQUIPMENT

Players must wear shirts, shorts, socks, shoes and shinguards. Teammates must wear matching colors, except for the goalkeeper, who must wear a different color of shirt than his teammates and of the referee.

Shoes may have non-metal studs or bars, either rounded or flat, and not less than one-half inch in diameter and not more than three-quarters of an inch in height. Molded studs must number at least 10, and be at least three-eighths of an inch in diameter.

Any equipment that might cause harm to another player is not permitted.

LAW V: REFEREES

The referee has complete authority to enforce the rules. The referee also keeps a record of the game and acts as timekeeper.

The referee may act on information from a neutral linesperson in making rulings. The referee can change a decision if play has not been restarted. If the referee determines that stopping play would give an advantage to a team committing a foul, play may continue. This decision is exhibited by shouting "Advantage, play on!"

The referee can caution (yellow card) or eject (red card) players, substitutes and team officials. The referee must report to the league all incidents of misconduct, before, during and after the game. One of the rules changes made in 1992 states that if a player receives two cautions in a game for offenses listed under Law 12, he must be sent off. In the past, a referee would show only the red card upon the second offense. Now both cards will be shown, indicating that the player was not sent off for an offense that required immediate ejection, but for two cautionable offenses.

The referee may stop the game for injuries or to end the game early to prevent disorder. If a game is ended early, the league determines the winner.

The referee determines who may enter the field of play, and prohibits coaching from the sidelines. (Some U.S. youth leagues permit limited coaching from along the sidelines.)

LAW VI: LINESPERSONS

Two linespersons assist the referee in controlling the game. The referee, however, has final authority and chooses whether or not to act on their advice.

Neutral linespersons signal a corner kick, a goal kick or a throw- in after the ball goes out of play. They also can signal offside violations, fouls and goals.

Club (non-neutral) linespersons, usually assigned by the two competing teams, signal only when the ball goes out of play.

LAW VII: DURATION OF THE GAME

The game is divided into two 45-minute halves. (Youth leagues and some American professional leagues play different lengths.)

The referee must extend the playing time for long delays in the game, such as substitution, injury, lost ball or time wasting by a team. The referee determines the amount of time to be added. If time has run out, it may be extended only for the completion of the kick.

Players are entitled to a halftime rest of at least five minutes.

LAW VIII: START OF PLAY

The referee and two team captains meet before the game to determine choice of ends and which team kicks off by the toss of a coin. The team winning the toss has the option of choice of ends or kicking off.

After the referee's signal, a player kicks the ball from the center of the field to the opponent's half of the field. All players must be standing in their respective half of the field not less than 10 yards from the ball.

The ball must travel forward the distance of its circumference. If it is kicked sideways or backward, it must be kicked over. The kicker may not touch the ball again until it has been touched by another player. Violations result in an indirect free kick for the opposing team. The ball may not be kicked off into the opposing team's goal. If it is, the other team restarts play with a goal kick.

After a goal has been scored, the game is restarted in a similar manner by a player on the team that has been scored against.

At the start of the second half, teams change ends and the kickoff is made by a member of the team that received the opening kickoff.

At the start of overtime, a coin is tossed. The team captain who wins the toss chooses either to kick off or defend a particular goal.

If play is stopped for a reason other than time running out or a rule being broken (an injury, for example), the referee restarts play by dropping the ball where the ball was at the time play was stopped. If the ball was in the goal area, however, the ball is dropped on the six-yard line at the point nearest where it was when play was stopped.

A drop ball is not in play until it hits the ground. If a player touches the ball before it hits the ground, it must be dropped again. Because the referee puts the ball into play, the first player to touch it may dribble, pass or shoot it.

LAW IX: BALL IN AND OUT OF PLAY

The ball is out of play when all of it has crossed the outside edge of the touch line or goal line, either on the ground or in the air. The ball is in play if it bounces off a goal post, crossbar or corner flag post and stays in the field of play, or when it strikes a referee or linesperson and stays in the field of play.

LAW X: METHOD OF SCORING

A goal is scored only if the entire ball crosses the outside edge of the goal line between the goal posts and crossbar and was not touched by the hand or arm of the attacking player.

A player who propels the ball into his own goal scores a goal for the other team, except when taking a free kick, throw-in, goal kick, penalty kick or kickoff.

LAW XI: OFFSIDE

A player is offside if he is nearer the opponent's goal line than the ball at the moment the ball is being played, unless:

1. He is in his own half of the field.
2. Two opponents (including the goalie) are nearer to the goal line.
3. The ball last touched an opponent.
4. He received the ball directly from a goal kick, a corner kick or a throw-in.

A player in an offside position is not called offside if he is not participating in the play or does not interfere with the opponent.

The position of a player at the moment the ball is played by a teammate determines whether the player is offside. If a player is onside at the moment the ball is played by a teammate, for example, he does not become offside by running to an offside position while the ball is in flight.

If a pass is intended for a teammate who is in an offside position and an opponent deflects the pass, offside still must be called because the offside occurred the moment the ball was played.

If a player is called offside, an indirect free kick is taken by the opposing team from the position of the offside player at the moment the ball was played.

LAW XII: FOULS AND MISCONDUCT

Some fouls result in a direct free kick or a penalty kick for the opposition. They are called if one of the following infractions is committed *intentionally* while the ball is in play:

1. Kicking or attempting to kick an opponent.
2. Tripping an opponent (even if the opponent does not fall down).
3. Jumping at an opponent (even if no contact is made).
4. Charging an opponent in a violent or dangerous manner.
5. Charging an opponent from behind, except when the player is legally obstructing the ball.
6. Striking, attempting to strike or spitting at an opponent.
7. Holding an opponent.
8. Pushing an opponent.
9. Touching the ball with the hands or arms, with the exception of a goalkeeper in his penalty area.

Other fouls result in an indirect free kick for the opposition. They are called if one of the following five infractions is committed while the ball is in play:

1. Dangerous play, such as kicking near an opponent's head or trying to play a ball held by a goalkeeper. If a player puts himself or herself in danger — such as by trying to head a low ball that the opponent is about to kick — the referee awards an indirect free kick to the opposing team.
2. Fair charging, which is shoulder-to-shoulder contact without danger to either player while the ball is out of playing distance (more than one step away).
3. Obstruction, such as intentionally getting in the way of the ball and the opponent when not within playing distance of the ball in an effort to prevent the opponent from playing the ball. Taking a position between the ball and the opponent while within playing distance is legal obstruction. It also is illegal for a player to use the body to block an opponent's movement.
4. Charging the goalkeeper, except when the goalkeeper is holding the ball, legally obstructing an opponent or when he has passed outside the goal area.
5. When goalkeepers take more than four steps while holding or bouncing the ball, or throw it in the air and catch it again before an opponent touches it. (Steps taken while trying to bring the ball under control are not counted.) If the goalkeeper releases the ball into play, he may not play it again until it has been played by a teammate outside of the penalty area or by an opposing player inside or outside the penalty area.

6. When goalkeepers handle a ball that is deliberately kicked by a teammate. This rule was added in 1992, and is perhaps the most important change ever made in the rules. Though intended to stop time wasting, the change also affects the way teams defend and attack. The goalkeeper cannot play a pass from a teammate with his hands, unless the ball, in the referee's judgement, was miskicked or deflected. (This rule change probably will spread defenses and encourage attacking soccer.)

Two kinds of misconduct penalties may be called: those resulting in a caution, and those resulting in ejection. When a referee cautions a player, he holds up a yellow card and records the player's number. The player may continue playing under a caution, but is ejected if another caution is issued. The referee raises a red card to signal that he is ejecting a player.

The following offenses result in a caution:

1. Entering or leaving the field without the referee's permission.
2. Persistently breaking the rules.
3. Showing by word or action dissent from a referee's decision.
4. Being guilty of ungentlemanly conduct, such as foul language, purposely delaying the game or committing hard fouls.

The following offenses result in ejection:

1. Serious foul play or violent conduct.
2. Using foul, insulting or threatening language.
3. Stopping a goal or an obvious scoring opportunity by deliberately fouling an opponent.
4. The referee may warn, caution or send off a player who is guilty of misconduct that happened while the ball was not in play, but the referee must not award a free kick for that misconduct.

LAW XIII: FREE KICK

Free kicks are classified as *direct* and *indirect*.

With a direct free kick, a goal can be scored by kicking a dead ball directly into the opponent's goal. It also counts as a valid goal if it touches a player from either team, except the kicker, on its way to the goal. This penalty is awarded after serious offenses.

An indirect free kick counts only if the ball is touched by another player on either team before passing into the goal.

In both cases, players from the opposing side must be at least 10 yards from the ball when it is kicked. The ball must be stationary when it is kicked. The ball is in play after it has traveled the distance of its own circumference. If the ball is played before it travels this distance, or before it leaves the kicking team's penalty area, the kick must be retaken.

Beginning with the rules changes enacted in 1992, free kicks may be taken from any place in the goal area.

The team taking a free kick inside its own penalty area is entitled to have all opponents at least 10 yards from the ball and outside the penalty area when the free kick is taken. The kicker may kick the ball without waiting. The same applies to free kicks taken outside the penalty area, except when the kick is taken within 10 yards of the opponent's goal, in which case opposing players can stand on their own goal line between the goal posts.

A player who delays taking a free kick is to be cautioned. A second offense results in ejection.

LAW XIV: PENALTY KICK

Fouls that would result in a direct free kick that occur inside the penalty box result in a penalty kick.

All players except the goalkeeper and the player taking the penalty kick must line up outside the penalty area, at least 10 yards from the ball. (This is the reason for the penalty arc.) The goalkeeper must stand on the goal line, between the goal posts, and not move his feet until the ball is kicked. If the goalkeeper moves his feet and the ball does not score, the kick is retaken.

No players may enter the penalty area or penalty area arc before the ball is kicked. This is called encroachment.

If a defender encroaches, the successful penalty kick is allowed while a non-scoring penalty kick is retaken.

If an attacker encroaches, a successful penalty kick is disallowed and the kick is retaken. A non-scoring shot that stays in play or is deflected out of play by the goalkeeper results in an indirect free kick for the defending team. A non-scoring shot that goes directly out of play results in a goal kick to restart the game.

If both an attacker and a defender encroach, the penalty kick is retaken whether it scores or not, and offenders are cautioned.

Penalty kicks must be played forward. Balls kicked sideways or backward are kicked again.

LAW XV: THROW-IN

A throw-in is made to restart the game after the ball completely crosses the touch line. It is taken from within one meter of where the ball crossed the line, by a member of the team opposite that of the player who last touched it.

The thrower must use both hands and deliver the ball from behind and over the head. The thrower, at the moment of delivering the ball, must face the playing field, and part of each foot must be on or outside the touch line.

The ball is in play after it enters the playing field, but the thrower may not play the ball again until it has been touched by another player.

If the ball is thrown improperly or from the wrong location, a player on the opposing team is awarded a throw-in. If the ball goes out of the playing field without being touched, the opposing team throws it in from where it crossed the touch line.

A player may not score by throwing the ball directly into the goal. If the ball is thrown into the opponent's goal, a goal kick is taken. If it is thrown into his or her own goal, a corner kick is taken.

A player who receives the ball directly from a throw-in while in an offside position is not offside.

LAW XVI: GOAL KICK

A goal kick is taken by a defending player after the ball goes out of bounds completely over the goal line but not into the goal, and was last touched by a member of the attacking team.

Beginning with the rules changes enacted in 1992, goal kicks may be taken from any place in the goal area. Players on the opposing team must remain outside the penalty area while the kick is being taken. If the ball does not go fully out of the penalty area, or if any players touch it before it leaves the penalty area, the kick shall be retaken. A goal cannot be scored directly from a goal kick. The ball must be stationary when kicked.

LAW XVII: CORNER KICK

A corner kick is taken by an attacking player after the ball goes out of bounds across the goal line, but not into the goal, and was last touched by a member of the defending team.

The entire ball must be placed within the quarter circle at each corner of the field. The corner flag posts may not be moved.

Opposing players must stand at least 10 yards away from the ball until it is kicked, unless the kicker chooses to kick the ball while they are closer. The ball is in play after it has traveled its own circumference. The kicker may not play the ball a second time until it has been touched by another player.

The corner kick may be taken by any player on the attacking team. A goal can be scored directly from a corner kick.

Part III: Information

Glossary

8

—A—

ADVANTAGE

When an apparent foul occurs, the referee has the option of calling it or not calling it. The decision is based on whether the player who fouled gained an advantage by making the foul. If he did not, no whistle results. Good referees will shout "Advantage, play on!" so that play continues without interruption.

ATTACK AREA

The third of the field of play in front of the goal being attacked. Sometimes called the attacking third or offensive third.

ATTACKING TEAM

The team with possession of the ball.

—B—

BACK

The general name given to a defender.

BENDING THE BALL

Making a pass, in the air or on the ground, where the ball swerves instead of travels in a straight line. The bending is made by putting side spin on the ball, much like hooking or slicing a golf ball.

BICYCLE KICK	See scissors kick.
BLADED	See chopped.
BLIND SIDE	The area of play that cannot be seen by a player or game official.
BRIDGING	Stooping in front of or behind an opponent in an effort to gain an advantage, usually on a high ball.
BLOCK TACKLE	A challenge for possession of the ball where the challenger, who is facing the ball dribbler, makes foot contact with the ball at the same time as the dribbler and tries to gain and maintain possession.
BOOKING	The referee's recording of a caution given to a player. It includes the player's shirt number and color, the nature and time of the offense, and any other pertinent information that might be useful in case of further review.
BUILT OFFENSE	A systematically developed attack, as opposed to a counterattack.

—C—

CATENACCIO	An extremely conservative, defensive style of play made famous by the Italian professional leagues. Now in disfavor because it lacks entertainment value and does not produce goals. Catenaccio means "padlock" in Italian; this style of play keeps the opponent imprisoned.
CAUTION	An official reprimand by the referee, given to a player who continually disobeys the game's laws, is unsportsmanlike, shows dissent by word or action from any decision given by the referee, or enters or leaves the field without the referee's permission. The referee signals a caution by raising a yellow card, and then records it. Further infractions result in a red card, and expulsion from the game.

CENTER

A pass that is made from a wide position on the field toward the center of the field, usually near goal.

CENTER CIRCLE

The area in which kickers from both teams must wait during the kicks from the penalty mark to break tied games. This circle marks the minimum distance that opposing team players must be from the team that kicks off.

CENTER FORWARD

The center player in the offensive attack. Also called a striker.

CHALLENGER

The player confronting an opponent, usually the dribbler, for the purpose of tackling him or containing him.

CHALLENGE SUPPORT

The defending player immediately behind the challenger for the ball.

CHARGE

See shoulder charge.

CHIP

A high pass over a defender's head to a teammate, or a shot on goal from close range away from the goalie's reach.

CHOPPED

Being tackled by a challenger who has intent other than obtaining possession of the ball. Also called "bladed." Can result in ejection if the referee considers it to be violent behavior.

CLEAR

Moving the ball out of a dangerous situation away from the attacking team.

CLOSE SUPPORT

Moving to aid a teammate to give him or her a passing option on attack or providing challenge support on defense.

COLLECT

To receive and control a pass.

COMBINATION PLAY

Passing between two or more players as they move toward the opponent's goal.

CONTAIN

A defensive tactic in which a challenger confronts the ball carrier without tackling him or her in order to slow the attacker or confine him or her to a non-dangerous area.

CORNER ARC
The area within which the ball must be placed to take the corner kick.

CORNER FLAGS
The flags located in the four corners of the field. A ball hitting the flag and remaining inbounds is in play. The flag may not be removed for corner kicks.

CORNER KICK
A direct free kick from the corner of the field, taken by the attacking team after the defense last played or touched a ball over the goal line.

COVERING
Providing support for a teammate challenging for the ball.

CROSS
A pass from one side of the field to the other, usually near the goal.

CROSSBAR
The horizontal piece of the goal posts, measuring 24 feet.

—D—

DANGEROUS PLAY
An action that could cause injury in the opinion of the referee. Examples are bringing the foot above shoulder level or dropping to head a low ball amid other players. The offending team loses possession of the ball and the opponent is awarded a free kick from the point of the infraction.

DASHER BOARDS
The wall forming the boundary of an indoor soccer playing area.

DEAD BALL
A ball not in play, either because it is outside the field of play or because the game has been temporarily suspended.

DECOY RUN
A movement by a player without the ball designed to draw the attention of an opponent away from the ball or player in possession.

DEFENSE
A team is playing defense whenever a member of the opposing team has control of the ball, regardless of field position.

DELIBERATE FOUL   Not to be confused with an intentional foul. A deliberate foul is more extreme and more planned than an intentional foul. Deliberate handling of the ball (such as catching it as a defensive measure), for example, is planned, against the spirit of the game and should result in a caution for the first offense. Intentional handling of the ball (such as purposely striking it with the hand) should be whistled, but the player normally should be penalized without a caution.

DIAGONAL SYSTEM   The universally accepted method of officiating, in which the referee runs on an imaginary diagonal from one corner of the field to the other, aided by two neutral linespersons with flags.

DIRECT KICK   A free kick that may be kicked directly into the opponent's goal. It scores even if it touches a player on either team on the way to the goal. Awarded to the opposing team as punishment for committing a penal foul.

DRIBBLE   To control the ball on the ground, with the feet. Not to be done excessively, and never when a pass or shot is an option.

DROP BALL   A ball dropped by the referee between two players after the game has stopped due to an injury, a foreign object on the field, or similar situations when no violation of the laws occurred, or when the referee is not certain who last touched the ball. Neither player can touch the ball until it has hit the ground.

DUAL SYSTEM   The two referee system of control, in which both referees have equal authority. No linesmen are used. This system is no longer approved by any national organizations.

DUMMY   A feinting movement to send a challenging opponent in the wrong direction. A decoy run is a form of dummy.

—E—

ENCROACHMENT
Ignoring the 10-yard distance an opponent must be from a free kick. Players usually are issued a caution for this offense.

END LINE
The entire goal line, from touch line to touch line.

—F—

FEINTING
A deceptive move by a player to disguise his or her real intention. A fake.

FIELD PLAYER
Any of the 10 players on a team other than the goalkeeper.

FLAT DEFENSE
A straight line of defenders, whereby a pass or a dribble through the line means instant penetration of the whole defense. Not recommended.

FORMATIONS
The alignment of players for strategic purposes. The goalkeeper is not included, because his position is fixed. Players located directly in front of the goalkeeper are listed first. The most common formations are 2-3-5, 4-2-4 and 4-3-3.

FORWARDS
The front line of a team, often consisting of an outside left and right (wings), inside left and right, and center forward.

FOUL
An infringement of the rules regarding behavior while the ball is in play. The referee usually judges fouls based on the intent of the one who fouled.

FREE KICK
An unchallenged kick awarded to a fouled team, taken from where the foul occurred (not necessarily from where the ball was at the time of the foul).

FRONT RUNNER
The most forward player on the attacking team. A term that describes a position in a tactical sense rather than a formal playing position.

FULLBACKS
The players who form the defense directly in front of the goalkeeper.

—G—

GOAL

(a) The area between the upright posts and under the crossbar, (b) the two posts and the crossbar themselves, and (c) a unit of scoring. A ball passing completely over the goal line and in the area termed the goal counts as a goal.

GOAL AREA

The area immediately in front of the goal, 20 × 6 yards in size.

GOAL KICK

An indirect free kick taken from the goal area to restart the game after the ball goes over the goal line when last being touched by an opposing player. Any player may make the kick, and it may be taken from any place in the half of the goal area on the side of the field where the ball went out of play.

GOAL LINE

The end lines extending from touch line to touch line, passing directly under the crossbars of the two goals.

—H—

HALFBACKS

The players who are the link between the fullbacks and the forwards. Often called "linkmen."

HALFWAY LINE

The line in the center of the field extending from touch line to touch line and dividing the field into two equal parts.

HALF VOLLEY

A kick made on the short hop. Goalkeepers sometimes drop-kick the ball; this is a half volley.

HEADING

Striking the ball with the head, usually the forehead.

HAT TRICK

Scoring three goals in a game.

HIDDEN FOULS

Fouls undetected by the referee, and therefore unpunished. They usually are committed by experienced players, and can lead to unpleasant incidents in a game.

HIGH KICKING

Raising the cleats near enough to another player to be judged as dangerous by the referee. Cleats are generally considered to be too high when they are above the waist, but it is up to the referee's discretion.

HITCH KICK

See scissor kick.

—I—

INDIRECT KICK

A free kick awarded for an opponent's infraction. After it is kicked, someone else on either team must touch the ball for a goal to be considered legal. Awarded for fouls, dangerous play, obstruction, and charging when the ball is not in playing distance.

INSIDES

The two players positioned on either side of the center forward, normally called the "inside right" and "inside left." As attackers, they are relied on for goals and for defensive help.

INJURY TIME

The time added to regulation time by the referee because of injury timeouts.

INSIDE-OF-THE-FOOT PASS

A ball kicked by striking it with the inside surface of the foot. The ball can be kicked straight or in a swerving path by brushing the ball with a hooking motion.

INSTEP PASS

A ball kicked by turning the toe downward and striking it with the instep (the top of the foot). The motion generally is used when shooting on goal, because it enables power and distance.

INTENTIONAL FOUL

A less severe infraction than a deliberate foul. The referee must determine the premeditation of the player. If a player willfully and repeatedly tries to gain an advantage by unfair means, then his acts are deliberate. If his violations are sporadic and generally non-disruptive, his acts are penalized, but not subject to disciplinary action.

—J—

JOCKEYING   Containing an opponent defensively while giving ground, either to wait for support, wait for an opportunity to challenge for the ball, or force the opponent to turn back. Also called shepherding or channeling.

—K—

KICKABOUT   An informal game of soccer, playing for exercise or for ball control and passing practice.

KICKOFF   The play that starts the game, the second half of a game or an overtime period, or restarts a game after a goal is scored.

—L—

LAWS OF SOCCER   The rules of the game, as established by FIFA, broken down into 17 laws.

LAW 18   An unwritten law used by referees to justify a decision that deviates from the laws of soccer, international board rulings, or common interpretations. It should be viewed as a "common sense law" pertaining only to those aspects and situations of the game not previously documented.

LINESPERSON   Referees with flags who usually signal for offside violations not seen by the referee, for balls out of bounds, and the direction for throw-ins. The senior linesperson, designated by the referee, takes over for the referee if needed, but has no decision-making authority otherwise. A linesperson can be neutral (having no affiliation with either of the teams playing in the game) or non-neutral (appointed by a participating club and called club linespersons).

LEAD PASS   A pass made ahead of the intended receiver that is measured to be taken in stride.

—M—

MARKING   A defensive duty of guarding an opponent.

MIDFIELDERS   A modern term applied to midfield players who link the forwards and defenders.

MISCONDUCT   An infringement of the Laws of the Game regarding behavior. Can occur while the ball is in or out of play. Includes dissent, frequent fouling, and ungentlemanly conduct.

MODIFIED DIAGONAL SYSTEM   A new system of game control that places three referees on the field, each with a whistle. It is generally acknowledged that fewer fouls occur in games whistled with this system.

—N—

NON-PENAL FOUL   Fouls usually considered to be less serious than penal fouls, punished by an indirect free kick. Non-penal fouls include dangerous play, charging without playing the ball, obstruction, charging the goalkeeper in the goal area when the goalkeeper does not have the ball, or time-wasting by the goalkeeper.

NUTMEG   Dribbling the ball through an opponent's legs and collecting the ball behind him.

—O—

OBSTRUCTION   The deliberate action of preventing another player's movement on the field. It is penalized by an indirect free kick. When the ball is within playing distance of the player who obstructs, the obstruction is legal.

OFFSIDE   A rules infraction in which an attacker does not have two or more opponents between him and the goal under attack when the ball is played toward him by a teammate. Exceptions to this rule exist; see Law XI for more information.

OFFSIDE POSITION　Being closer to the opponent's goal than the ball while the ball is being played, while: (1) in the opponent's half of the field, and (2) having fewer than two opponents between oneself and the goal line. The offside position does not become "offside" until the player participates in or interferes with play. Offside is not called on a corner kick, goal kick, throw-in, or drop ball.

OFFSIDE TRAP　A difficult defensive maneuver designed to place an attacking player offside just before an attacker plays the ball. Successful execution requires perfect timing from the defense.

OUTSIDE-OF-THE-FOOT PASS　A ball kicked by striking it with the outside surface of the foot. The ball travels in a slicing path away from the foot.

OUTSIDES　The two forwards on the outside of the field, close to the touch line. They usually take the corner kicks, and often are the fastest players on the team, so they can outrun the fullbacks for the ball. Also called "wings" or "wingers."

OVER THE BALL　The dangerous act of raising one's foot above and over the ball in a manner that when an opponent attempts to kick the ball, or follow through on a kick, he is likely to be severely cleated in the shin. This is the worst foul in soccer, and should not be tolerated by referees.

OVERLAP　The action of a defender who comes from behind and goes on an attacking run past his midfield or forward players.

—P—

PENAL FOULS　The nine fouls that result in a direct free kick, or a penalty kick if the foul is made in the penalty area. Penal fouls include pushing, tripping, holding, kicking or attempting to kick, striking or attempting to strike, hand ball, charging an opponent violently or dangerously, jumping at an opponent, and charging an opponent from behind.

PENALTY ARC

The arc at the top of the penalty area. No player other than the kicker may be in this area when a penalty kick is being taken. It is not a part of the penalty area, so a penal foul within it is not punishable by a penalty kick.

PENALTY AREA

The area in front of the goal, 18 × 44 yards in size. The goalkeeper may legally handle the ball in this area. All "direct" fouls by the defense in this area result in penalty kicks rather than direct free kicks.

PENALTY KICK

A direct free kick from the penalty mark given to the attacking team for a penal foul against the defending team in the defending team's penalty area. The kick is taken 12 yards from the goal, on the penalty mark. Penalty kicks are about 90 percent successful.

PENALTY MARK

The mark in the penalty area from which a penalty kick is taken.

PITCH

A British term for a soccer field.

POINT MAN

A player who stays barely onside, receives passes and distributes the ball to teammates to penetrate a defense.

PUSH PASS

A straight pass made by striking the ball with the inside surface of the foot, with no bending motion. The most accurate method of passing, but generally practical only for short distances.

QUARTER CIRCLE

The corner area, from which corner kicks are taken.

QUICK KICK

A free kick taken immediately following the referee's whistle for the foul, designed to prevent defenses from being set up against the free kick.

—R—

RECOVERY RUN
The return, usually at a sprint pace, to a player's normal position. Usually occurs after a dribbler loses possession of the ball and must take up emergency defensive duties. Also might be required of an overlapping player who did not receive a pass.

RED CARD
The card used by a referee to signal that a player has been ejected from a game.

REFEREE
The individual appointed to officiate a soccer game.

REGULATION TIME
For adult men's games, 90 minutes — two 45-minute halves. Varies for women's and youth games. Time is kept on the sideline by a timekeeper in high school. Otherwise it is kept by the referee, who can add time to cover injury timeouts, time wasting, or other reasons.

—S—

SANCTIONED
Penalized.

SANDWICHING
Two teammates converging on an opponent simultaneously. This type of "boxing in" is penalized with a direct free kick, as it is regarded as holding.

SAVE
A stop by a goalkeeper of an attempt on goal.

SCISSORS KICK
An acrobatic move whereby the player jumps and twists his or her body so that the feet are over the head, then strikes the ball with a hitching motion. This attempt is judged dangerous play and results in an indirect free kick if the referee considers it to be dangerous to an opponent. This is true even if no contact was made with the opponent, and the intent was to kick the ball.

SCREENING
A player positioned between the ball and a challenger, to prevent the challenger from getting to the ball. This is legal movement, provided the ball is within playing distance of the screener. If not, the move is an obstruction, a non-penal foul.

SHORT CORNER	A corner kick taken by sending it to a nearby teammate rather than directly to the goal. Useful in junior-level games, where the kicker might not have the power to send the ball into the goal area, where the defense has a superior air game, or to provide an element of surprise.
SHOULDER CHARGE	Using a shoulder against an opponent's shoulder to gain an advantage. A legal maneuver, as long as the ball is within playing distance (three feet), and being played. The charge must be done nonviolently.
SLIDE TACKLE	Stripping the ball from a dribbler by making contact with the ball while sliding on the turf. It is a foul if contact is first made with the dribbler, or if the action is deemed dangerous to the dribbler.
SOLE TRAP	Stopping the ball between the ground and the sole of the shoe.
SQUARE PASS	A lateral pass to a teammate, going neither forward nor backward.
STOPPER	A defender whose main role is to shut down attacks. The last defender before the goalkeeper.
STRIKER	A player whose main job is to score goals. Normally a forward, although any player attempting to score may be considered a striker.
SWEEPER	A roving defender who plays behind the fullbacks and is the safety valve defender who "sweeps up" balls that are played past them.

—T—

TACKLE	To take the ball away from an opponent by using the feet. Can be done while standing or sliding.
THROUGH PASS	A pass sent through a defense for a receiver to run after and collect in the space behind a defense. Sometimes called a "killer" pass.

THROW-IN

The method of returning the ball to play after it has gone over the touch line and was last touched by an opponent. This is the easiest skill to perform in soccer, yet often the most poorly executed.

TIME WASTING

Delaying the restart of the game after the ball is dead. If the ball is not in play, the referee can caution for the delay. If the ball is in play, the referee can award an indirect free kick and a caution against the offending team.

TOUCH LINE

The line marking the side of the field, named as such because after the ball passes outside it the player may touch (handle) the ball. Throw-ins are taken from touch lines from the place where the ball left the field of play.

TRAPPING

Getting the ball under control by using any part of the body except the hands.

—V—

VIOLENT CONDUCT

Intentional rough play that should carry both technical and disciplinary sanctions.

VOLLEY

Playing the ball with the foot before the ball reaches the ground.

—W—

WALL

A group of at least three defenders standing shoulder-to-shoulder to defend a free kick, usually near the goal. The human "wall" must be 10 yards from the ball, or on the line between the goal posts.

WALL PASS

A pass made to a second surface (another player) with an expected return pass, as with a "give-and-go" in basketball.

WARNING   A verbal admonition given by the referee to the player
                              who is guilty of some infringement of the laws. If the
                              infringement is repeated, a caution (yellow card) usu-
                              ally results.

—Y—

YELLOW CARD   The card used by a referee to signal that a player has
                              received an official caution.

—Z—

ZONE DEFENSE   A defensive strategy in which players are assigned to
                              areas, rather than to specific players.

 **9**

Directory

Organizations

AMATEUR ATHLETIC UNION
David B. Morton, Director of Communications
3400 W. 86th St.
P.O. Box 68207
Indpls. IN
46268
(317) 872-2900

Ken Houser, National Soccer Chairman
2230 Toronado Ct.
Clearwater, FL
34623
(813) 734-4215

AMERICAN ATHLETIC ASSOCIATION FOR THE DEAF
Shirley H. Platt, Executive Director
3607 Washington Blvd.
Ogden, UT
84403
(801) 393-7916

AMERICAN PROFESSIONAL SOCCER LEAGUE
Emily J. Ballus, Director of Operations
Donn Risolo, Media Relation Director
4300 Fair Lakes Court
Suite 300-B
Fairfax, VA
22033
(703) 222-2403

AMERICAN YOUTH SOCCER ORGANIZATION
Lolly Keys, Director
5403 W. 138th St.
Hawthorne, CA
90250
1-800-USA-AYSO

ATHLETES IN ACTION
Elsie S. Fadner, Director of Soccer
7899 Lexington Dr.
Suite 200
Colorado Springs, CO
80920
(719) 593-8200

CONCACAF
(Confederation Norte-Centroamericana y Del Caribe de Footbal)
717 Fifth Ave., 13th Floor
New York, NY
10022
(212) 308-0044

FIFA
(Federation Internationale de Football Association)
P.O. Box 85
8030 Zurich
Switzerland
01/384 95 95 (phone number)

INTERCOLLEGIATE SOCCER ASSOCIATION OF AMERICA
Jack Writer, President
Box 729
Ithaca, NY
14851
(607) 255-8467, day
(607) 257-0829, evening
Men's rating recorder: (314) 984-0516
Women's rating recorder: (314) 984-0611

MAJOR SOCCER LEAGUE

Vince Fiduccia, Director of Communications
120 E. Baltimore St.
Suite 2150
Baltimore, MD
21202
(410) 347-7622

NATIONAL ASSOCIATION OF INTERCOLLEGIATE ATHLETICS

1221 Baltimore Ave.
Kansas City, MO
64105
(816) 842-5050

NATIONAL COLLEGIATE ATHLETIC ASSOCIATION

6201 College Blvd.
Overland Park, KS
66211-2422
(913) 339-1906

NATIONAL PROFESSIONAL SOCCER LEAGUE

Paul Luchowski, Director of Operations
229 Third St. NW
Canton, OH
44702
(216) 455-4625

NATIONAL SOCCER COACHES ASSOCIATION OF AMERICA

James Shelton, Executive Director
4220 Shawnee Mission Parkway
Suite 105B
Fairway, KS
66205
(800) 458-0678

SOCCER ASSOCIATION FOR YOUTH

James Gruenwald, Executive Director
4903 Vine St.
Cincinnati, OH
45217
(800) 233-7291

SOCCER INDUSTRY COUNCIL OF AMERICA

Sandy Briggs, Executive Director
200 Castlewood Dr.
North Palm Beach FL
33408
(407) 840-1171

SOCCER SOLIDARITY, INC.

David Vowell, VP/Director of Communications
1307 Howard Rd.
Glen Burnie, MD
21060-7404
(410) 766-6065

SOCCER START

(inner city soccer program)
TJ Kostecky, Chairman
New Jersey Institute of Technology
University Heights
Newark, NJ
07102
(201) 596-3633

SPECIAL OLYMPICS INTERNATIONAL

Mike Smith, Director of Soccer
1350 New York Ave., NW
Suite 500
Washington, D.C.
20005

UNITED STATES AMATEUR SOCCER ASSOCIATION

Fritz Marth, Administrator
7800 River Rd.
North Bergen, NJ
07047
(201) 861-6277, day
(201) 338-6153, evening

UNITED STATES SOCCER FEDERATION

John Polis, Director of Communications
1801-1811 S. Prairie Ave.
Chicago, IL
60616
(312) 808-1300

UNITED STATES YOUTH SOCCER

2050 N. Plano Rd.
Suite 100
Richardson, TX
75082
(800) 4-SOCCER

WORLD CUP USA, 1994, INC.
Jim Trecker, VP/Press Officer
1270 Avenue of the Americas
Suite 220
New York, NY
10020
(212) 332-1994

Publications

SOCCER AMERICA
P.O. Box 23704
Oakland, CA
94623-0704
(415) 528-5000

SOCCER INTERNATIONAL
P.O. Box 246
Artesia, CA
90702-0246
(310) 860-9252

SOCCER JOURNAL
Official Publication of the National Soccer Coaches
Association of America
West Gymnasium
SUNY-Binghamton
Binghamton, NY
13902-6000
(607) 777-2133

SOCCER JR.
The Soccer Magazine for Kids
27 Unquowa Rd.
Fairfield, CT
06430

Museum

NATIONAL SOCCER HALL OF FAME
5-11 Ford Ave.
Oneonta, NY
13820
(607) 432-3351

PHOTO COURTESY ST. LOUIS UNIVERSITY

Indiana University's Jerry Yeagley, left, and St. Louis University's Bob Guelker, above, have coached two of the most successful college soccer programs in history. Indiana won the NCAA championship in 1982, '83 and '88 and was runnerup in 1976, '78, '80 and '84. Guelker's teams at St. Louis won championships in 1959, '60, '63 and '65, and finished second in 1961. Both coaches are members of the National Soccer Hall of Fame.

PHOTO BY KENT PHILLIPS

Champions

World Cup Champions

Year	Final game	Host city
1930	Uruguay 4, Argentina 2	Montevideo, Uruguay
1934	Italy 2, Czechoslovakia 1	Rome, Italy
1938	Italy 4, Hungary 2	Paris, France
1950	Uruguay 2, Brazil 1	Rio de Janeiro, Brazil
1954	West Germany 3, Hungary 2	Berne, Switzerland
1958	Brazil 5, Sweden 2	Stockholm, Sweden
1962	Brazil 3, Czechoslovakia 2	Santiago, Chile
1966	England 4, Italy 2	London, England
1970	Brazil 4, Italy 2	Mexico City, Mexico
1974	West Germany 2, The Netherlands 1	Munich, West Germany
1978	Argentina 3, The Netherlands 1	Buenos Aries, Argentina
1982	Italy 3, West Germany 1	Madrid, Spain
1986	Argentina 3, West Germany 2	Mexico City, Mexico
1990	West Germany 1, Argentina 0	Rome, Italy

Olympic Champions

Year	Final game	Host city
* 1900	United Kingdom 2, Denmark 0	Paris, France
* 1904	Canada 4, U.S. 0	St. Louis, Mo.
* 1906	Denmark 9, Greece 0	Athens, Greece,
1908	United Kingdom 2, Denmark 0	London, England,
1912	United Kingdom 4, Denmark 2	Stockholm, Sweden
1920	Belgium 2, Czechoslovakia 0	Antwerp, Belgium
1924	Uruguay 3, Switzerland 0	Paris, France
1928	Uruguay 2, Argentina 1	Amsterdam, Holland
1936	Italy 2, Austria 1	Berlin, Germany
1948	Sweden 3, Yugoslavia 1	London, England
1952	Hungary 2, Yugoslavia 0	Helsinki, Finland
1956	USSR 1, Yugoslavia 0	Melbourne, Australia
1960	Yugoslavia 3, Denmark 1	Rome, Italy
1964	Hungary 2, Czechoslovakia 1	Tokyo, Japan
1968	Hungary 4 Bulgaria 1	Mexico City, Mexico
1972	Poland 2, Hungary 1	Munich, West Germany
1976	East Germany 3, Poland 1	Montreal, Canada
1980	Czechoslovakia 1, East Germany 0	Moscow, Russia
1984	France 2, Brazil 0	Los Angeles, Ca.
1988	USSR 2, Brazil 1	Seoul, South Korea

* — Unofficial competition

NCAA Champions
Men
Division I

Year	Champion	Score	Runner-up
1959	St. Louis	5-2	Bridgeport
1960	St. Louis	3-2	Maryland
1961	West Chester	2-0	St. Louis
1962	St. Louis	4-3	Maryland
1963	St. Louis	3-0	Navy
1964	Navy	1-0	Michigan St.
1965	St. Louis	1-0	Michigan St.
1966	San Francisco	5-2	LIU-Brooklyn
1967	*Game between Michigan St. and St. Louis called due to bad weather*		
1968	*Maryland and Michigan St. tied, 2-2, in two overtimes*		
1969	St. Louis	4-0	San Francisco
1970	St. Louis	1-0	UCLA
1971	vacated		St. Louis
1972	St. Louis	4-2	UCLA

1973	St. Louis	2-1 (ot)	UCLA
1974	Howard	2-1 (4ot)	St. Louis
1975	San Francisco	4-0	SIU-Edwardsville
1976	San Francisco	1-0	Indiana
1977	Hartwick	2-1	San Francisco
1978	vacated		Indiana
1979	SIU-Edwardsville	3-2	Clemson
1980	San Francisco	4-3 (ot)	Indiana
1981	Connecticut	2-1 (ot)	Alabama A&M
1982	Indiana	2-1 (8ot)	Duke
1983	Indiana	1-0 (2ot)	Columbia
1984	Clemson	2-1	Indiana
1985	UCLA	1-0 (8ot)	American
1986	Duke	1-0	Akron
1987	Clemson	2-0	San Diego St.
1988	Indiana	1-0	Howard
1989	*Santa Clara and Virginia tied, 1-1, in two overtimes*		
1990	UCLA	1-0 (4ot, pk)	Rutgers
1991	Virginia	0-0 (pk)	Santa Clara

Division II

1972	SIU-Edwardsville	1-0	Oneonta St.
1973	Missouri-St. Louis	3-0	Cal St. Fullerton
1974	Adelphi	3-2	Seattle Pacific
1975	Baltimore	3-1	Seattle Pacific
1976	Loyola, Maryland	2-0	New Haven
1977	Alabama A&M	2-1	Seattle Pacific
1978	Seattle Pacific	1-0 (2ot)	Alabama A&M
1979	Alabama A&M	2-0	Eastern Illinois
1980	Lock Haven	1-0 (ot)	Florida International
1981	Tampa	1-0 (ot)	Cal St.—L.A.
1982	Florida Int.	2-1	Southern Conn. St.
1983	Seattle Pacific	1-0	Tampa
1984	Florida Int.	1-0 (ot)	Seattle Pacific
1985	Florida Int.	3-2	Florida Int.
1986	Seattle Pacific	4-1	Oakland
1987	Southern Conn. St.	2-0	Cal St.—Northridge
1988	Florida Tech	3-2	Cal St.—Northridge
1989	New Hamp. College	3-1	N.C.—Greensboro
1990	Southern Conn. St.	1-0 (4ot,pk)	Seattle Pacific
1991	Florida Tech	5-1	Sonoma State

Division III

1974	Brockport St.	3-1	Swarthmore
1975	Babson	1-0	Brockport St.
1976	Brandeis	2-1 (2ot)	Brockport St.
1977	Lock Haven	1-0	Cortland St.
1978	Lock Haven	3-0	Washington (Mo.)
1979	Babson	2-1	Glassboro St.
1980	Babson	1-0 (ot)	Scranton
1981	Glassboro St.	2-1 (4ot)	Scranton
1982	N.C.-Greensboro	2-1	Bethany (W. Va.)
1983	N.C.-Greensboro	3-2	Claremont
1984	Wheaton (Ill.)	2-1 (3ot)	Brandeis
1985	N.C.-Greensboro	5-0	Washington (Mo.)
1986	N.C.-Greensboro	2-0	UC San Diego
1987	N.C.-Greensboro	6-1	Washington (Mo.)
1988	UC San Diego	3-0	Rochester Inst.
1989	Elizabethtown	2-0	Greensboro
1990	Glassboro St.	2-1 (4ot,pk)*	Ohio Wesleyan
1991	UC San Diego	1-0	Trenton State

Women
Division I

Year	Champion	Score	Runner-up
1982	North Carolina	2-0	Central Florida
1983	North Carolina	4-0	George Mason
1984	North Carolina	2-0	Connecticut
1985	George Mason	2-0	North Carolina
1986	North Carolina	2-0	Colorado College
1987	North Carolina	1-0	Massachusetts
1988	North Carolina	4-1	North Carolina St.
1989	North Carolina	2-0	Colorado College
1990	North Carolina	6-0	Connecticut
1991	North Carolina	3-1	Wisconsin

Division II

1988	Cal. St. Hayward	1-0	Barry
1989	Barry	4-0	Keene State
1990	Sonoma State	2-0	Keene State
1991	Cal St. Dominguez Hills	2-1	Sonoma State

Division III

1986	Rochester	1-0	Plymouth State
1987	Rochester	1-0	William Smith
1988	William Smith	1-0	UC San Diego
1989	UC San Diego	3-2 (3ot)	Ithaca
1990	Ithaca	1-0 (4ot, pk)*	Cortland State
1991	Ithaca	2-0	Rochester

* pk — penalty kick

NAIA Champions

Men

Year	Champion	Score	Runner-up
1959	Pratt Institute, NY	4-2 (2ot)	Elizabethtown, PA
1960	*Elizabethtown and Newark Engineering, NJ tie (2-2,4ot)*		
1961	Howard	3-2	Newark Engineering
1962	East Stroudsburg, PA	4-0	Pratt Institute
1963	*Earlham, IN and Castleton State, VT, tie*		
	(game cancelled because of snow)		
1964	Trenton State, NJ	3-0	Lincoln, PA
1965	Trenton State, NJ	6-2	Earlham, IN
1966	Quincy, IL	6-1	Trenton State, NJ
1967	Quincy, IL	3-1	Rockhurst, MO
1968	Davis & Elkins, WV	2-1 (5ot)	Quincy, IL
1969	Eastern Illinois	1-0 (2ot)	Davis & Elkins, WV
1970	Davis & Elkins, WV	2-0	Quincy, IL
1971	Quincy, IL	1-0	Davis & Elkins, WV
1972	Westmont, CA	2-1 (ot)	vacated
1973	Quincy, IL	3-0	Rockhurst, MO
1974	Quincy, IL	6-0	Davis & Elkins, WV
1975	Quincy, IL	1-0	Simon Fraser (BC, Canada)
1976	Simon Fraser	1-0	Rockhurst, MO
1977	Quincy, IL	3-0	Keene State, NH
1978	Quincy, IL	2-0	Alabama- Huntsville
1979	Quincy, IL	1-0	Rockhurst, MO
1980	Quincy, IL	1-0 (ot)	Simon Fraser
1981	Quincy, IL	4-1	Alderson-Broaddus, WV
1982	Simon Fraser	4-0	Midwestern State, TX
1983	Simon Fraser	1-0	Midwestern State, TX
1984	West Virginia Wesleyan	3-2 (2ot)	Fresno Pacific, CA
1985	West Virginia Wesleyan	4-3 (4ot)	Fresno Pacific, CA
1986	Sangamon State, IL	1-0	Simon Fraser
1987	Boca Raton, FL	1-0 (ot)	Simon Fraser

1988	Sangamon State, IL	3-1	Alderson- Broaddus, WV
1989	West Virginia Wesleyan	1-0	Boca Raton, FL
1990	West Virginia Wesleyan	3-1	Boca Raton, FL
1991	Lynn University **	2-1 (ot)	Midwestern State, TX

** — formerly Boca Raton

Women

Year	Champion	Score	Runner-up
1984	St. Mary's, CA	4-0	Cardinal Newman, MO
1985	Westmont, CA	4-2	Puget Sound, WA
1986	St. Mary's, CA	3-0	Berry, GA
1987	Berry, GA	1-0	Erskine, SC
1988	Pacific Lutheran, WA	2-0	Hardin-Simmons, TX
1989	Pacific Lutheran, WA	2-1	Berry, GA
1990	Berry, GA	3-1, (2ot)	Pacific Lutheran, WA
1991	Pacific Lutheran, WA	4-0	Missouri Valley, MO

Hall of Fame

The National Soccer Hall of Fame was established in 1950 by the Philadelphia Soccer Old Timers Association as a means of honoring those people who have made outstanding contributions to soccer in the United States. It had honored 194 men and women as of 1992.

The Hall inducted its first 50 members between 1950 and 1953. The U.S. Soccer Federation has assumed the role of selecting inductees since 1953. In 1982, the National Soccer Hall of Fame joined the USSF in recognizing the inductees in its national museum in Oneonta, N.Y.

As of 1992, the following people had been voted into the Hall of Fame:

DR. JOHN J. BROCK (1950): Captain and coach of the first soccer team at Springfield College, Mass. in 1906. During his regime as coach, Springfield won the national championship twice, and the New England intercollegiate title four times.

ANDREW M. BROWN (1950): Secretary of the USSFA from 1924 to 1926, and its president from 1926 to 1928. Goodwill ambassador to many foreign countries.

THOMAS W. CAHILL (1950): Secretary of the USSFA from 1913-1921, and 1923-24. Manager of U.S. soccer teams that played in Norway, Denmark and Sweden from 1916-1920.

JOHN "JOCK" FERGUSON (1950): Former Scottish and English professional. Played left fullback for North End, Arborath, St. Johnstone and Dundee F.C. Came to U.S. and played nine years for Bethlehem Steel.

WILLIAM GONSALVES (1950): American-born player and record holder of medals won in the National Challenge Cup. Played forward for Fall River 1930-31, also with New Bedford, Stix Baer and Fuller, and Brooklyn. Played on U.S. teams that toured Rome, Mexico, Germany and Haiti.

SHELDON GOVIER (1950): Played center halfback for Pullman F.C. of Chicago for several years. Played with the All-Stars of Chicago that defeated the Pilgrims of England. Also excelled in baseball, rugby and boxing.

GEORGE "BARNEY" KEMPTON (1950): Played with some great teams in Belfast, Ireland. Came to the U.S. and played in Los Angeles and Seattle. Was secretary and junior commissioner of the Washington state association.

MILLARD LANG (1950): Played for Cantons of Baltimore, Graphite Bronze of Cleveland and Sparta S.C. of Chicago. Coached Towson (Md.) Juveniles. Also wrote for *Soccer News.*

HORACE EDGAR LEWIS (1950): Born in Wales and came to this country at the age of 14. Became vice president of Bethlehem Steel Co. and organized for that company the nation's greatest soccer team in the early 20th century. Donated the Lewis Cup for competition.

DR. G. RANDOLPH MANNING (1950): Became first president of the USFA in 1913. President of the NYSA from 1928 to 1948. Chairman of the Foreign Relations Committee in 1948. First American to be a council member of the International Federation.

ROBERT MILLAR (1950): Played with St. Mirren F.C. of Scottish League. Emigrated in 1911 and played with Tacony, Brooklyn, Bethlehem Steel, Babcock and Wilcox, Robbins Dry Dock and the New York Giants. Coached the U.S. team that played in Montevideo (1930), and played for the U.S. in 1925 against Montreal, Canada.

HARRY RATICAN (1950): Learned to play soccer in St. Louis. Played for Ben Millers from 1911 to 1915. Played for Bethlehem Steel from 1915 to 1919. Also played with Fall River, Robbins Dry Dock and Todd's Ship Yard. Varsity soccer coach at West Point, N.Y.

ARCHIE STARK (1950): Emigrated from Scotland in 1912 at the age of 12. Was the greatest goal scorer of his time. Played with Scottish-Americans, West Hudsons, Bethlehem Steel, and Fall River. Toured Sweden and Denmark in 1919. Played for the U.S. against Canada in 1925-26. Toured Czechoslovakia, Austria, Yugoslavia and Hungary in 1930.

DOUGLAS STEWART (1950): Became first president of Thistle F.C. in Philadelphia in 1903. Organized and became Secretary of the Football Association of Pennsylvania. Organized and became president of the Referee's Association of Pennsylvania. Head coach at University of Pennsylvania from 1910 to 1942, and vice president of the USFA in 1921-22.

PETER WILSON (1950): Played with St. Johnstone of the Scottish League in 1896-97. Emigrated to America in 1898 and played with Scottish-Americans, Paterson Rangers, Pawtucket of Rhode Island and Hibernians of Philadelphia.

GEORGE HEALEY (1951): Born in England. Later moved to Detroit and organized the Michigan State Association. President of the USFA from 1919 to 1923.

PETER RENZULLI (1951): Native-born goalkeeper for the famed Robbins Dry Dock, New York Nationals, and New York Giants teams. Considered by many as one of the greatest of all native-born goalkeepers. Also an organizer and promoter of youth soccer.

PETER J. PEEL (1951): Born in Ireland. Later an outstanding athlete in Chicago. Past president of the USFA. Donated famous Peel Cup in 1909, which is still in competition.

JAMES McGUIRE (1951): Born in Scotland. Played pro soccer in Scotland and England. Came to the U.S. and played in the American league with the Celtics and Brooklyn. Became President of the American League in 1946, and was first vice-president of the USSFA.

JOHN A. FERNLEY (1951): Active in soccer for many years in New England. Past president of the USFA.

THOMAS SWORDS (1951): Born in Fall River, Mass. Played with Fall River, Hibernians and New Bedford. Considered by many the greatest native-born center forward. Captained All- American team which toured Scandinavia.

HAROLD BRITTAN (1951): Born in England. Played for Derby County and Chelsea 1st Division. Came to U.S. and played for the great Bethlehem Steel and Fall River teams. Regarded by many as one of the greatest center forwards to play in the United States.

CHARLES "DICK" SPAULDING (1951): Played in Philadelphia, Densington, Victor, Disston and Bethlehem. Considered by many the greatest native fullback of his day. Played in Norway and Sweden. Professional baseball outfielder with Philadelphia and Washington.

GEORGE M. COLLINS (1951): Born in Scotland, and came to the U.S. in 1908. Played here, and later became prominent organizer. Managed U.S. Olympic team in Paris in 1924. Officer of USSFA, and Soccer Editor for The Boston *Globe* from 1914 to 1950.

JOHN McGUIRE (1951): A clever, aggressive inside forward. Played in Scotland, England and Canada. Came to U.S. in 1922, played for Todd's, New Bedford, Brooklyn and for the U.S. National Team against Canada.

ALFREDDA INGLEHART (1951): From Baltimore. First woman admitted to the Hall of Fame. Taught and coached soccer teams for 30 years. Many of her pupils became star players. Also coached baseball, basketball, and track.

WILLIAM JEFFREY (1951): Born in Scotland. Later played in U.S. Took over as head coach at Penn State in 1926. Had 13 undefeated seasons and a run of 65 games without a defeat. Coach of the 1950 U.S. World Cup team that defeated England 1-0.

ROBERT MORRISON (1951): Born in Scotland. Came to the U.S. in 1910. Played for Tacony and the great Bethlehem Steel team. Stopped playing in 1918 after a knee injury. A great team player at halfback.

WILLIAM FRYER (1951): Born in England. Played for Newcastle and Barnsley. Came here in 1920, played until 1935 with Todd's, Fall River, and the N.Y. Giants. A rugged, hardnosed player and a great center halfback.

ELMER A SCHROEDER (1951): Managed many outstanding championship teams. President of USSFA 1933-34. Managed U.S. World Cup Team in Italy in 1934, the Olympic team in Berlin in 1936, and the National team in Mexico in 1937.

EDWARD J. DONAGHY (1951): Born in Scotland, played with Tacony, Hebs, and Bethlehem. A fine player and later an outstanding referee. President of New York Referee's Committee, and chairman of Arbitration Board.

ALFRED A. SMITH (1951): Played at Springfield College. Coach and physical fitness director at Germantown Friends School, Philadelphia starting in 1914. An outstanding coach who won 15 championships. Editor of the *National College Soccer Guide.*

DENT McSKIMMING (1951): Born in St. Louis. Began career as soccer writer in 1922. Covered games in Mexico City in 1949, Rio De Janeiro in 1950. Followed sports in South America and Cuba.

DAVID BROWN (1951): A great player of the 1920s. Fast ball control and terrific shot. Played for Erie, Newark and New York Giants. Played in Canada and Sweden. A great outside left.

RUDDY EPPERLEIN (1951): Born in Germany. Active in playing and promotion of soccer around Buffalo, New York for 25 years. A great worker for soccer.

JOSEPH TRINER (1951): Connected with soccer for 25 years. Past president of USSFA, chairman of the Illinois Soccer Committee, and chairman of the State Athletic board controlling all athletics in Illinois.

JOSEPH BOOTH (1952): Born in Bradford, England. Secretary of the Connecticut State Association for 25 years. Third vice president of USSFA from 1920 to 1923, and a member of the National Cup Committee.

WILLIAM PALMER (1952): Born in England. Officer of various leagues and chairman of USSFA finance committee in Philadelphia. Amateur teams compete annually for William Palmer Memorial Cup.

ERNO SCHWARZ (1952): Born in Budapest, Hungary. Came to U.S. with famous Hakoah All-Stars in 1926, stayed here and played with many teams. Career ended in 1937 with a broken leg. Business manager of the American League, and owner/manager of the NY Americans.

JAMES ARMSTRONG (1952): Born in Carlisle, England. Secretary of New York state association. Executive Secretary of USSFA from 1931 to 1944. Manager of U.S. Olympic team in 1936.

JACK JOHNSTON (1952): Born in Glasgow, Scotland. Was a soccer referee for 20 years and a soccer reporter for the *Chicago Tribune* for 30 years.

HARRY FAIRFIELD (1952): Born in England. Player, referee and officer in West Penn district for many years. President of USSFA from 1945 to 1948. Sports reporter for the *Pittsburgh Press*. Died at the age of 100.

JOHN W. WOOD (1952): Born in England and played for Fulham, London. President of Illinois Referee's Association and successful high school coach. Chairman of National Junior Cup. Coached U.S. Olympic team in 1952.

GEORGE TINTLE (1952): Born in Harrison, N.J. An outstanding goalkeeper who played in international matches abroad against Norway, Sweden and Denmark. Also a successful high school soccer coach.

POWYS A.L. FOULDS (1953): Born in England, player and manager. Came to Canada, then to U.S.. Noted legislator was member of 1928 Olympic committee and president of State Assn. A consulting engineer.

WILFRED CUMMINGS (1953): Born in Chicago. Secretary-Treasurer of state association and Peel Cup for more than 30 years. Treasurer USSFA from 1923 to 1931. Managed 1930 World Cup team in Uruguay. Was Executive Secretary to Chief Justice Municipal Court, Chicago.

JOHN JAAP (1953): Born in Scotland. Excellent player with Castle Shannon and other Pittsburgh area teams. Inside right for eight years with Bethlehem Steel. Later coached junior teams.

JOHN J. MacEWEN (1953): Born in Canada, then moved to Cleveland where he became a player and legislator. President of state association and secretary of national Amateur Cup. Interested in junior promotion. Devoted a lifetime of unselfish service to game.

JOHN MARRE (1953): Player and manager in his youth. Did much to keep the sport alive around St. Louis. Member of the Missouri state commission and National Challenge Cup commission.

DAVID L. GOULD (1953): Born in Scotland. An outstanding player and assistant coach at University of Pennsylvania for 28 years. Coached U.S. World Cup team in 1934. Also president of Referee's Association.

JOSEPH J. BARRISKILL (1953): Born in Ireland. Player and manager in his youth. President of USSFA from 1932 to 1934. Manager of 1948 Olympic team. Delegate to FIFA 1948. Chairman of National Cup commission 1928 to 1940.

PAUL KLEIN (1953): Born in Egypt. Played soccer in Germany before coming to U.S. in 1923. Played for and managed the Elizabeth, N.J. soccer club from 1939 to 1952. Won many championships in various competitions.

ALDO DONNELLI (1954): Scored only U.S. goal in 1934 World Cup game in Italy. After prominent playing career, became well-known collegiate and professional football coach.

JAMES DOUGLAS (1954): Member of 1924 Olympic team and 1930 World Cup team. Later a top player with various pro clubs.

JAMES "JIMMY" MILLS (1954): Coached Haverford & Girard College and later the Philadelphia Nationals, the four-time ASL champs. As coach of the 1956 Olympic team, brought back the first winning record for a U.S. soccer team in Olympic competition.

THOMAS DUGAN (1955): Player on four New Jersey and two New York state championship teams and one National Open Cup winning team.

EDGAR POMEROY (1955): A year after his arrival from England in 1889, he had already organized two soccer teams. Formed the first San Francisco Bay area team. Key figure in the history of California soccer.

WILLIAM ANDERSON (1956): A top administrator in Southern New York State soccer as well as a president of various leagues.

VICE WESTON (1956): Washington state area top soccer player and later an administrator in the Texas area. Known as the "Father of Texas Soccer."

VERNON REESE (1957): Began affiliation with soccer in 1914 as a player in the 60-pound class. Professional player, manager and coach in Baltimore soccer. Ran annual soccer clinics for many years.

CHARLES FERRO (1958): Well-known writer for Spanish newspaper *La Prensa*. Also a longtime referee.

FRED NETTO (1958): USSF President from 1951 to '53. Longtime secretary of the Illinois Soccer Association. Held many key USSF positions. Top figure in Chicago soccer.

FRANCIS "HUN" RYAN (1958): Regarded as one of the greatest dribblers in U.S. soccer history. Member of the 1928 Olympic Team and the 1934 World Cup team. Longtime star of the ASL Philadelphia German-Americans.

JOHN YOUNG (1958): A force in California soccer as an organizer, innovator, teacher, and player.

RALPH CARRAFI (1959): Outstanding West Penn player. A Cleveland pro at outside left position during the 1930s, and a top referee.

ROBERT CRADDOCK (1959): A National Cup commissioner, top administrator, and key figure in Pittsburgh soccer.

EMIL SCHILLINGER (1960): Earned national fame as manager and administrator of Philadelphia German-Americans club, a top team of the 1930s and early 40s.

MATTHEW BOXER (1961): President of the Northern California Soccer Association. Devoted more than half a century to soccer as a player, coach, and administrator. District commissioner of the USSF.

WILLIAM HEMMINGS (1961): President of the National League from 1946 to 1961. An all-star halfback in English soccer who played for many different teams throughout the U.S.

WALTER GEISLER (1962): Manager of the U.S. team that defeated England in the 1950 World Cup. Former vice- president and president of the USSF. An Olympic soccer coach, and prominent in three decades of Missouri soccer.

HARRY KRAUS (1963): Was the youngest vice president in USSF history. Spent 15 years as New York State Association secretary. Also German-American League president and manager of USSF 50th anniversary gala.

RUDY KUNTNER (1963): Olympian and National Open Cup champion team member in 1939. Played for 1947 Brookhattan team which won National Cup, American League Cup, and Lewis Cup.

DIMITROS NIOTIS (1963): National chairman of USSF Youth and School Promotion Committee. Author and Illinois high school coaches Man of the Year in 1973. A life member of the Chicago National League.

DANIEL ZAMPINI (1963): Pittsburgh soccer standout and later president of West Penn Soccer Federation. Vice-chairman and chairman of the National Amateur Cup Committee.

JACK FLAMHAFT (1964): Founded National Soccer League in New York. President of American Soccer League and a driving force for more than 30 years for the New York Hokoah team. USSF President from 1959 to 1961.

PRUDENCIO "PETE" GARCIA (1964): Member of FIFA and a top referee. Officiated 1950 World cup final. Player, coach, and organizer throughout the rank of Missouri soccer.

OSCAR KOSZMA (1964): Dubbed the "Godfather of Soccer" in Los Angeles. A player, coach, and administrator through many years at all levels of California soccer.

FRED BEARDSWORTH (1965): Won NCAA Award of Merit in 1964. A renown player, manager, and innovator.

CHARLES GLOVER (1965): Member of the 1928 National Challenge Cup teams. Starred on ASL and German-American League clubs. Performed in many international all-star games.

STANLEY CHESNEY (1966): For almost two decades, a goalkeeper for the N.Y. Americans, winners of the National Challenge Cup in 1937 and other soccer championships.

MAURICE HUDSON (1966): A leading personality in California soccer and an all-star player and administrator. Held executive posts with San Francisco leagues and the California state association.

COLIN COMMANDER (1967): The "Father of Ohio Soccer" was active at all levels. National Cup commissioner from 1950 to 1957.

HARRY "PUP" FLEMING (1967): A key figure in starting the Hall of Fame through the Philadelphia Old-Timers' Association. A player, owner, and manager at various levels of Pennsylvania soccer.

WILLIAM MORRISSETTE (1967): Played a major role in the organization of the New England Soccer League. A Fall River area player, executive, National Cup commissioner, and soccer media specialist.

WALLY PETERS (WALTER PARICCIUOLI) (1967): Active in soccer for more than 50 years. Was chairman of the New Jersey state soccer association. Director of Kearny (NJ) Scots all-star team during their five-year championship streak.

JOHN DRESMICH (1968): A leading figure in West Penn soccer as a player and manager. Was chairman of the West Penn commission from 1955 until his death in 1968.

ARNOLD OLIVER (1968): An outstanding scorer on the 1926 Amateur Cup champs. A member of the first U.S. World Cup team in 1930.

TOM SAGER (1968): Was USSF president from 1941 to 1945, vice president from 1939 to 1941. A former Hall of Fame Selection Committee chairman.

FRED SHIELDS (1968): An Olympic team member, and for 30 years a high school and college referee. Member of the Kearny (NJ) Scots, who won five straight championships. Paced his college team to four years of undefeated play.

EDMUND CRAGGS (1969): Former secretary/treasurer for the Washington state association. First non-Catholic in the U.S. to receive the Pro Deo Et Juventute award for CYO coaching.

S.T.N. "SAM" FOULDS (1969): Historian for the Hall of Fame, organizer and president of the Massachusetts Bay State League. Brandeis University soccer coach. Recipient of National Soccer Coaches' Certificate of Merit.

AUGUST STEUR (1969): Internationally known soccer figure and former president of the German-American League. Honorary commissioner for public events in New York City for Mayors Wagner and Lindsay.

DANIEL FOWLER (1970): American-style soccer product. Was a high echelon New York state soccer administrator. The Northwestern State Junior Cup is named for him.

JACK MAHER (1970): Organizer, manager, and referee for games involving top pioneer teams, such as the Thistles, Sparta and Swedish-Americans. A leading personality in Illinois soccer.

GENE OLAFF (1971): Premier goalkeeper of his time. Paced the National Challenge Cup wins of the Brooklyn Hispanos in 1943 and 1944. Was a member of the 1939 National League Cup Hatikvah team.

BERTRAND PATENAUDE (1971): Standout player who was member of the first U.S. World Cup team in 1930. Played on four National Challenge Cup championship teams.

UMBERTO ABRONZINO (1971): A respected personality as a player and administrator in the world of California soccer.

JOHN ARDIZZONE (1971): A respected personality as a player and organizer at several levels of soccer.

ALLAN McCLAY (1971): An administrator, referee and longtime soccer personality in northern Massachusetts and New Hampshire.

PETER A. MEROVICH (1971): Member of West Penn and Keystone League all-star teams. Also a referee and administrator for West Penn soccer. Commissioner for National Amateur, Open, and Junior Cups.

MILT MILLER (1971): Outstanding soccer journalist and one-time part owner of N.Y. Hakoah-Americans. Publisher of *Soccer News.*

JAMES F. MOORE (1971): An administrator holding all levels of appointment at all levels of soccer in St. Louis.

JACOB "JACK" ROTTENBERG (1971): Contributed more than six decades of service to U.S. soccer as a coach, manager, and administrator. Won six state titles and the Lewis Cup in 1944.

NICOLAAS STEELINK (1971): Active for more than 50 years in soccer as a player, official and referee. A founder of the California Soccer League.

ROBERT STONE (1971): Longtime figure active at all levels of soccer in Colorado and its neighboring states.

JAMES WALDER (1971): Organizer of USSF and dean of U.S. referees. Officiated over 5,000 games from 1909 to his retirement in 1969.

JULIUS ALONSO (1972): Almost 70 years of dedication and service to soccer as a player, manager, referee, league secretary and archivist. Dubbed "Mr. American Soccer League."

DUNCAN DUFF (1972): Longest term of service of any president in southern California soccer history. All-star right halfback who helped develop soccer on the West coast.

JOSEPH GRYZIK (1973): Top Chicago area player noted for gentlemanly play and for never being ejected from a game.

JOSEPH DELACH (1973): Administrator in West Penn soccer and outstanding amateur player.

GEORGE FISHWICK (1974): Three-time president of Illinois Soccer Association, two-time president of the USSF, FIFA, CONCACAF delegate, and one-time owner/publisher of *National Soccer News*.

WERNER MIETH (1974): Played soccer for more than 40 years. Won many medals, championships, and titles. Coached various levels in New Jersey.

NICK DIORIO (1974): Played in many National Cup games during the 1940s. Was a top goalkeeper in West Penn soccer.

JAMES DUNN (1974): A native of St. Louis, he was a top amateur and professional player.

ALEX WEIR (1975): Active for more than 50 years in soccer. Played and coached many teams at all levels. President of the National League and executive of the German-American League.

TED CORDERY (1975): Longtime outstanding personality in San Francisco soccer as an amateur player and administrator.

WALTER BAHR (1976): An All-American, Olympian, and member of the 1950, '54 and '58 World Cup teams. A longtime Penn State University soccer coach.

CHARLES COLOMBO (1976): His key tackle as a member of the 1950 World Cup team safeguarded a victory over England. A two-time Olympian, he represented the U.S. in over 100 international matches.

JOE GAETJENS (1976): Scored the lone goal in the U.S. 1950 World Cup upset over England. Was the ASL Leading scorer in 1950 with the N.Y. Brookhattans.

HARRY KEOUGH (1976): A top amateur and professional player in St. Louis National and International soccer. Was a member of the 1950 U.S. World Cup team, and later a successful coach at St. Louis University.

ED McILVENEY (1976): Member of the 1950 World Cup team and a former outstanding Scottish professional player. Starred at many different levels of soccer in Pennsylvania.

JOSEPH MACA (1976): Member of the 1950 World Cup team, and played with Swiss F.C. of German-Americans and Brooklyn Hispanos of the ASL. Was a member of several all-star teams, and was the ASL Most Valuable Player in 1950.

GINO PARIANI (1976): Member of the 1950 World Cup team and a top player in the St. Louis area.

GIORGIO PISCOPO (1978): Founder and former president of the N.Y. Italian-American Soccer League. A star left-winger during his playing days.

LAWRENCE BRIGGS (1978): A past president of the National Soccer Coaches' Association of America and an innovator in education and sports. He was secretary of the Intercollegiate Soccer Football Association and New England Intercollegiate Soccer League. An award is named in his honor at the University of Massachusetts.

ENZO DELUCA (1979): No information available.

ALBERT HARKER (1979): Member of the 1934 World cup team and the first German-American team in the ASL (1933-34). Selected for the 1936 Olympic team. Won eight trophies in ASL regular season play.

KURT LAMM (1979): Played fullback and forward for 29 years, and coached for 14 years. Was president of the ASL from 1962 to 1967.

J. EUGENE RINGSDORF (1979): Paved the way for soccer in U.S. schools. Played for 20 years in the Baltimore area. Won the Stewart Cup in 1937 and was president of the USSF from 1954 to 1961.

JOHN "FRENCHY" BOULOS (1980): Nicknamed the "Pocket Rocket." A star player with such teams as the Bay Ridge Hearts, Degura, Brooklyn Hispano, and Hakoah. Born in Haiti, he came to the U.S. in 1925 and was active in the ASL Former Players Association.

ROBERT GUELKER (1980): A coach from 1958 to 1972 at St. Louis University and SIU-Edwardsville. Coached over 300 collegiate wins, and was coach of the winning Olympic soccer team in 1972 in Munich, Germany.

DR. G.K. "JOE" GUENNEL (1980): Called "Father Soccer." Was the secretary of the NSCAA in 1962. Played 10 years and coached for 30. Known for promotion, development and administration of soccer, he was inducted in 1980.

GEORGE CRAGGS (1981): A halfback who he played amateur soccer for 16 years. He coached four years and was a USSF National referee for 23 years. Also served as USSA and USSRA referee coordinator.

ERWIN SINGLE (1981): A respected soccer journalist and administrator. Was president of the USSF from 1969 to 1971, vice president from 1963 to 1969, and editor of the *ASL Soccer News*. Did Monday night broadcasts of games for 20 years.

HARRY JOHN SAUNDERS (1981): Over 30 years of service to soccer, played with HOTA one year and for 10 years was its secretary and vice president. Was president of the German-American League for nine years, and active in several other soccer organizations.

JOHN O. BEST (1982): Played 10 years for Chicago area clubs, including Schwagen, Ulster, UTD, Carpenter's, and Sloboda. A FIFA referee of special distinction. Served 13 years as USSF vice president.

JOSEPH CARENZA (1982): No information available.

LAMAR HUNT (1982): Owner of the Dallas Tornado, an original charter member of the NASL. Also active in World Championship Tennis. An inductee of the football Hall of Fame in Canton, Ohio.

GEORGE BARR (1983): Nicknamed "Gentleman George." Regarded as the best defender in the ASL. Was captain of the Brookhattan Soccer Club. A triple crown winner (ASL, Lewis Cup and National Challenge Cup) and representative of the ASL.

FRANK KRACHER (1983): Played with Fichte Soccer Club as a goalie from 1946 to 1960. Held various administrative duties with the National Soccer League and USSF.

ERNEST FEIBUSCH (1984): No information available.

RAYMOND GRANVILLE KRAFT (1984): Noted player from 1928 to 1948, and referee from 1948 to 1978. Later held many positions in soccer activities.

GUISEPPE LOMBARDO (1984): Founder of the Italian-American Soccer League, despite never having played. Has been the registrar and senior administrator of the Southern NYS Soccer Association since 1969.

GENE EDWARDS (1985): USSF president from 1974 to 1984. Manager for Pan-American and Olympic soccer teams in 1971-72. Member FIFA Amateur Committee and Executive Committee of the U.S. Olympics.

DON GREER (1985): No information available

ANDREW AULD (1986): Member of the 1930 U.S. World Cup team that competed in Uruguay. Also played in the Providence area.

MICHAEL BOOKIE (1986): Member of the 1930 U.S. World Cup team. Played professionally in the Cleveland area.

JAMES BROWN (1986): Member of the 1930 U.S. World Cup team. Also played for the New York Giants soccer club. Played professionally for Manchester United and Glasgow Celtic.

THOMAS FLORIE (1986): Member of the 1930 and 1934 World Cup teams. Also played in the New Bedford and Pawtucket areas.

JAMES GALLAGHER (1986): Member of both the 1930 and 1934 World Cup teams. Also played in the Cleveland area and for the New York Nationals.

JAMES GENTLE (1986): Member of the 1930 World Cup team that competed in Uruguay. Also played for teams in the Philadelphia area.

BART McGHEE (1986): Member of the 1930 World Cup team. Also a player for the New York Nationals.

GEORGE MOORHOUSE (1986): Played on the 1930 and 1934 World Cup teams. Also played for teams in the New York City area.

PHILIP SLOAN (1986): Played for the 1930 World Cup team and various New York City teams.

RAPHAEL "RALPH" TRACEY (1986): Member of the 1930 World Cup team. Also played for the Ben Millers team with Hall of Famer Frank Vaughn.

FRANK VAUGHN (1986): Member of the 1930 World Cup team. Also played for Ben Millers with World Cup teammate Ralph Tracey.

ALEXANDER WOOD (1986): Member of the 1930 World Cup team. Also played for the Holly Carburetors.

JOHN "JACK" COLL (1986): Assistant manager for the 1930 World Cup team.

MIKE KABANICA (1987): Played soccer in Yugoslavia, Italy, and Austria before coming to the U.S. in 1950. Played, coached and managed the Milwaukee Serbians. Later became president of the Wisconsin Soccer Association.

DON PHILLIPSON (1987): Served as Colorado State Soccer Association secretary and completely revised the organization and structure of the state governing body. USSF vice president from 1975 to 1977. Chairman of the USSF Referee Committee and helped structure and develop a national referee development program still in existence.

THOMAS E.A.H. WEBB (1987): Began career in England as a goalkeeper in the Isthmian League. Came to U.S. in 1966. Involved in every aspect and level of administration. President of Washington State Soccer Association and USSF vice president. Refereed ASL and NASL games. Chairman of USSF National Referee Committee. Involved in youth soccer, coached and conducted numerous clinics.

HERBERT HEILPERN (1988): Former president of the Blue Star Sport Club and German-American Soccer League. Co-founder of the NASL and the New York Cosmos team. Soccer coordinator of the City of New York, president of GASL Junior League and vice-president of Eastern New York Youth Association.

BERTIL A. LARSON (1988): Coached and played for Hartford Scandia for over 20 years. Held numerous positions in the Connecticut Soccer Association and other leagues. Was soccer editor of the *Hartford Courant* for more than 25 years.

JERRY YEAGLEY (1989): Began coaching at Indiana University in 1963, when the sport was at the club level. After soccer became varsity sport at I.U. in 1973, built it into a national power. Has won three national championships and numerous national coaching honors.

WERNER ROTH (1989): A standout athlete in his school years. He served as captain of the New York Cosmos for three of his eight years there. He also was captain of the U.S. National Team and Director of the Special Olympics from 1982 to 1987.

ROBERT GORMLEY (1989): Product of Philly's Lighthouse Boy's Club. Played with the first German-American team of the ASL for 17 years, spending 12 as their captain. Chosen for the U.S. national team for 1954 World Cup matches.

WILLY ROY (1989): Played for U.S. national team from 1965 to 1973, including preliminary games for three World Cups. Played pro for Chicago Spurs and Sting. Also coached Sting. Served as head coach of Northern Illinois University.

WALTER DICK (1989): Played in the ASL for Providence, Pawtucket Rangers and Kearny Scots. The latter team won five successive national championships. He played on the 1934 World Cup team and the 1935 U.S. select team in Mexico.

GEORGE DONNELLY (1989): Extremely active as an administrator, he served as President of the NSL and founded the ENYYSA. He served on numerous USSF committees and was a member of the Board of Directors.

SHAMUS O'BRIEN (1990): Signed with the ASL New York Giants in 1924 at the age of 17. A prolific scorer, he played in many international matches against some of the best teams in the world. Helped lead his team to three ASL crowns.

BOB KEHOE (1990): Player in the St. Louis Pro League. The first American-born coach in the NASL with St. Louis Steamers. Captain of the U.S. national team in 1965 and coach of the team in 1972. The director of coaching at Busch Soccer Club.

EDDIE PEARSON (1990): Organizer and chief referee for NASL. Was CEO of the NASL in 1968. Developed Georgia state and national referee progams. CONCACAF referee instructor in 1974. Developed USSF referee courses.

MANFRED SCHELLSCHEIDT (1990): Played in West Germany, and both the ASL and NASL in the U.S. Holder of West German DFB license. Coached U.S. national and youth teams, Olympic and Pan-American teams, MISL and NASL teams and Seton Hall University.

MILTON AIMI (1991): Served in the highest echelons of Houston area soccer. USSF vice president in 1982 and again in 1988. Among his other USSF positions: chairman of the Senior Division and the Amateur Division.

RUDY GETZINGER (1991): Began playing with the junior team of Schwaben A.C. in Chicago. A four-time member of the Olympic team and a member of the U.S. national team from 1970 to 1972, playing over 50 games.

EFRAIN "CHICO" CHACURIAN (1992): Signed professional contract at the age of 15 in Argentina. Moved to New York in 1947 and played with the New York Armenian Soccer Club. Led team to league championship and was voted league MVP. Signed with Hispano Club of the ASL in 1949, and was selected to U.S. National Team that year. Selected to the 1950 U.S. World Cup team, but was unable to play. Later coached Bridgeport City Soccer Club and at Southern Connecticut State College, Yale and University of Bridgeport. Also active in Olympic Development Program.

WERNER FRICKER (1992): Native of Yugoslavia who moved to Austria at the end of World War II and emigrated to the U.S. in 1952. Played professionally for 23 years, and a member of the 1964 U.S. Olympic team. Led the United German Hungarians to several amateur championships between 1954 and 1969. Captain of the team that won the national amateur title in 1965, and advanced to the finals in 1964 and '66. An active administrator, he was elected President of the USSF in 1984, and was responsible for bringing the 1994 World Cup to the U.S. Later served on board of directors for World Cup '94 Organizing Committee, Inc. and on executive committee of CONCACAF.

RON NEWMAN (1992): A native of Portsmouth, England and a player for 13 years in the British leagues. Came to the U.S. in 1967 and began professional career. The all-time winningest coach in North American soccer, and the only one to reach the 500-win plateau. Had record of 625-387-27 as of early 1992. Coach of the Major Soccer League's San Diego Sockers for the past 12 years, winning 10 championships. Coached the MSL's Western Division all-star team for eight consecutive years. Has a 323-189 record in MSL play. Named the league's Coach of the Year in 1987-88 after leading team to a 42-14 record. Has also won titles in the NASL indoor and outdoor leagues, and the ASL. Innovative coach who invented the "super power play," removing the goalkeeper in favor of a sixth attacker, and revolutionized the concept of changing lines, situating the players on the bench so they can get into their proper positions on the field faster.

Bibliography

Cirino, Tony. *U.S. Soccer vs. the World.* New Jersey: Damon Press, 1983.

Harris, Paul and Sam Foulds. *America's Soccer Heritage. A History of the Game.* California: Soccer for Americans, 1979.

Pronk, Nick, and Barry Gorman. *Soccer Everyone.* North Carolina: Hunter Textbooks, 1991.

Rosenthal, Gary. *Everybody's Soccer Book. New York: Charles Scribner's Sons, 1981.*

Rote, Kyle Jr., with Basil Kane. *Kyle Rote, Jr.'s Complete Book of Soccer.* New York: Simon and Schuster, 1978.

USSF Official Publication. *World Cup Italia '90.* Finland: Commemorative Soccer Publications, 1990.

About the Author

This is Paul Harris' 18th book on soccer. His writings for coaches, players, referees, spectators, parents and historians have inspired and challenged almost a million readers. He has refereed more than 2,000 times, and claims to learn something new in each game. He lives in Manhattan Beach, California.

MASTERS PRESS

DEAR VALUED CUSTOMER,

Masters Press is dedicated to bringing you timely and authoritative books for your personal and professional library. As a leading publisher of sports and fitness books, our goal is to provide you with easily accessible information on topics that interest you written by the most qualified authors. You can assist us in this endeavor by checking the box next to your particular areas of interest.

We appreciate your comments and will use the information to provide you with an expanded and more comprehensive selection of titles.

Thank you very much for taking the time to provide us with this helpful information.

Cordially,
Masters Press

Areas of interest in which you'd like to see Masters Press publish books:

☐ COACHING BOOKS
    Which sports? What level of competition?

☐ INSTRUCTIONAL/DRILL BOOKS
    Which sports? What level of competition?

☐ FITNESS/EXERCISE BOOKS
    ☐ Strength—Weight Training
    ☐ Body Building
    ☐ Other

☐ REFERENCE BOOKS
    what kinds?

☐ BOOKS ON OTHER
    Games, Hobbies
    or Activities

Are you more likely to read a book or watch a video-tape to get the sports information you are looking for?

I'm interested in the following sports as a participant:

I'm interested in the following sports as an observer:

Please feel free to offer any comments or suggestions to help us shape our publishing plan for the future.

Name _____ Age _____

Address _____

City _____ State _____ Zip _____

Daytime phone number _____

BUSINESS REPLY MAIL

FIRST CLASS MAIL   PERMIT NO. 1317   INDIANAPOLIS IN

POSTAGE WILL BE PAID BY ADDRESSEE

MASTERS PRESS

2647 WATERFRONT PKY EAST DR DEPT WF

INDIANAPOLIS IN 46209-1418

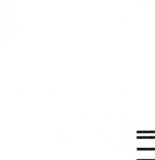